The Christian Sunday Calendar. This observ Franicevich's typological approach to Sunday observance. Far more than a New Testament command to abstain from kinetic activity, the Sunday turns out to be a multifaceted version of Sabbath, Passover, and Firstfruits—all wrapped into one. *Sunday* is a biblical theological study in the best sense of the term, paying careful attention to the biblical text while at the same time being deeply concerned with the worshipful lives of contemporary Christians. Writing in crystal-clear, sparkling idiom, Franicevich challenges us to reject Pharaoh and all his host, so that instead we may entrust ourselves to the God who sets us free.

Hans Boersma
Saint Benedict Servants of Christ Chair in Ascetical Theology
Nashotah House Theological Seminary

Creative, bold, pastorally rich: Franicevich delivers a wonderful reflection on the Christian's "festal" identity. With a keen and expansive Scriptural reach, he outlines a humble appropriation of Israel's Sabbath, Passover and the feast of the First Fruits (Shavuot or Weeks) into the Christian's Sunday Eucharist, showing how this can serve as center of our reception of Jesus' transformative offering of His own patrimony. This work of exegesis, imaginative exploration, and passionate moral encouragement is a gift to pastors, ministers and all faithful followers of Christ.

Ephraim Radner
Professor of Historical Theology
Wycliffe College, University of Toronto

Time is the liturgically ordered cadence and rhythm which structures our experience of the real world. It belongs to the creative and providential works of God and derives its form and contours from the form of the Son Himself. He is Lord of time and wisely, lovingly exercises that Lordship by shaping His people through and in terms of time. However--though this may sound provocative—time may also be the arena of His Lordship against which even His own people most frequently rebel.

With characteristic generosity paired with relentless pursuit of the real world of Holy Scripture, Jack Franicevich draws us into the colorful and rich world of Luke's Levitical Sabbath theology. Jack's commendation of the Sabbath as neither a moral, ceremonial, nor judicial law as such but as the most conspicuous feature in the biblical and Christian metaphysic of time provokes truly edifying—and potentially revolutionary—self-examination regarding how time is providentially purposed to form, free, and fill us. Refreshingly, Jack's own voice is heard throughout this study, and for those who know him this only deepens the delight this book is. His mature reflections on the Lord's ordering of His people through time arises from his own experience of the Lord's grace to him in this area. This, then, is no mere apologia but an invitation to a blessing Jack has himself come to know and continues to learn. I would like to join him in his invitation. I fully expect you to do the same upon reading this lively little book.

Mark A. Garcia
President; Fellow in Scripture & Theology
Greystone Theological Institute

After exploring the liturgical stories behind the Old Testament Sabbath in my own work, I was thrilled to read Jack's book on the liturgical storytelling behind the New Testament Lord's Day! And what a timely book this is! In a society filled with stress and tension, Sunday calls us to Christ's gift of rest. Written with both pastoral care and theological carefulness, this book explores the beauty of the Sabbath principle throughout Scripture—particularly as it emerges in the New Testament church. And more importantly, this book helps us envision how this practice can reframe our own hectic lives within a liturgy of rest, today.

Michael Lefebvre
Presbyterian Minister; Fellow
The Center for Pastor Theologians

SUNDAY

SUNDAY

KEEPING CHRISTIAN TIME

JACK FRANICEVICH
S.T.M., Nashotah House

THEOPOLIS EXPLORATIONS
LITURGY 2

Theopolis
BOOKS
AN IMPRINT OF ATHANASIUS PRESS

Sunday: Keeping Christian Time

Theopolis Books

Copyright © 2023 by Jack Franicevich
Published by Theopolis Books
An Imprint of Athanasius Press

Athanasius Press
715 Cypress Street
West Monroe, Louisiana 71291
www.athanasiuspress.org

Cover design: Ryan Harrison
Typesetting: Christopher D. Kou

ISBN: 978-1-957726-11-3

All rights reserved. No part of this publication may be reproduced, stored in a retrieval system, or transmitted in any form or by any means—electronic, mechanical, photocopy, recording, or any other—except for brief quotations in printed reviews, without the prior permission of the publisher.

This publication contains The Holy Bible, English Standard Version®, copyright by Crossway Bibles, a publishing ministry of Good News Publishers. The ESV® text appearing in this publication is reproduced and published by the cooperation between Good News Publishers and Athanasius Press and by permission of Good News Publishers. Unauthorized reproduction of this publication is prohibited.

The Holy Bible, English Standard Version (ESV) is adapted from the Revised Standard Version of the Bible, copyright Division of Christian Education of the National Council of the Churches of Christ in the U.S.A. All rights reserved.

English Standard Version®, ESV®, and the ESV® logo are trademarks of Good News Publishers located in Wheaton, Illinois. Used by permission.

To St. John's Anglican Church in Petaluma, CA, which raised me as a child and taught me the indelible lesson—through truly hour-long coffee hours, park picnics, volleyball games, and house parties—that Sunday was special.

To God who "concealed the matter" and to the teachers who helped me to "search it out."

THEOPOLIS EXPLORATIONS
SERIES INTRODUCTION

The Theopolis Institute is a community of pastors, theologians, and students devoted to articulating, disseminating, and implementing a Trinitarian vision of the church's mission that centers on deepening the church's understanding in Scripture and her faithfulness in liturgical practice. The church carries on her world-transforming mission by being the church. When the church inhabits the symbolic world of the Bible through the liturgy, sings Psalms, and communes together at the Lord's table, the Spirit of Christ makes her what she in fact is—the light and life of the world.

Theopolis teaches, develops tools, and fosters networks to assist church leaders throughout the world to form biblically-grounded and liturgically-vibrant catholic churches. The Theopolis Institute is not a church, but like scaffolding to assist the body and bride of Christ as she builds the heavenly city that transforms the cities of man.

The Theopolis Explorations Series builds on the four volumes of the Theopolis Fundamentals Series. Each Explorations volume brings the Theopolitan vision to bear on a particular biblical, liturgical, cultural, or missional topic. Theopolis Explorations are well-researched but not academic, elegantly but not popularly written, thorough but not exhaustive. The authors do not claim to speak the final word on the issues they examine, but aspire to offer a helpful word to strengthen and embolden the church as she carries on the mission of King Jesus in today's world.

For more information about Theopolis, visit our web site, TheopolisInstitute.com.

CONTENTS

Foreword — xiii

Acknowledgements — xv

Introduction — 001

Chapter 1: Big Sabbath — 008

Chapter 2: Your Holidays — 027

Chapter 3: Sabbath Hero — 050

Chapter 4: Passover President — 080

Chapter 5: Luke's First Day — 108

Chapter 6: The Substance — 131

FOREWORD

PETER J. LEITHART

Bible. Liturgy. Culture. It's the Theopolis triad. And Jack Franicevich's study of Sunday is a thoroughly Theopolitan achievement.

Start with Bible. Jack provides a deft overview of Israel's Sabbath and her Sabbatical calendar. He accentuates the social and economic import of Sabbath laws, so dreadfully ignored among Sabbatarians throughout history (yes, I'm referring to Presbyterian slaveholders in the Old South). In Luke's Gospel, Jack discovers a "liturgical historiography" that reveals a Jesus who carries out His ministry under the banner of the Big Sabbath (Luke 4; Isa 61, with Lev 25 in the background), complete with seven Sabbath episodes.

Then Liturgy. Sunday is the church's transfigured Sabbath—at least that. Sunday is our commemorative holiday, a day to celebrate the resurrection of Jesus that fulfills the Sabbath, the Passover, and, Jack demonstrates, the Feast of Firstfruits. The Lord's service recalls and enacts the year of release Jesus announced in Nazareth and achieved at Easter. The absolution is a liberating declaration of forgiveness. Preaching is festal speech. The Eucharist transposes the liturgical timekeeping of Israel into a new key. Sunday is for discerning and rebuking Pharaonic powers, for forgiving, and for pursuing restitution. Sunday-keeping must extend beyond Sunday to generate a Sabbatical ethos that extends release even to enemies.

Finally, Culture. This is perhaps the most innovative part of Jack's project. He takes a cue from Eugen Rosenstock-Huessy, who suggested that true citizens are those who have the capacity to recreate a civilization in the event of its collapse. Holidays form just such citizens. They're seasons of gratitude for what the Lord has done and given. Because holidays commemorate defining moments of our history, they're also occasions for critique, as we measure our national life by reference to what our holidays teach us to aspire to. Jack encourages us to observe the federal calendar, not in a perfunctory manner, but as a way of becoming the kinds of citizens who can reproduce American civilization if it should fall into ruins.

Sorting these topics into distinct categories obscures the intricate message of this book. We distort the meaning of Sunday if we separate biblical from liturgical from cultural concerns. The biblical Sabbath and calendar shapes the liturgical life of Israel and the church, and by shaping liturgical time, the biblical Sabbath and calendar set the time signature of cultural time.

To discern the meaning of Sunday, to grasp any theological topic, we need to do what Jack has done so well here. We must recognize how Bible, Liturgy, and Culture are knotted up together, inseparably, perichoretically entwined. Theology can't be done properly any other way.

Holy Week 2023
Beth-Elim
Gardendale, Alabama

ACKNOWLEDGEMENTS

I want to begin by thanking the people who taught me how to read the Bible and write about it. Especially Peter Leithart who, at a pivotal time in my education, apprenticed me one-on-one in reading the gospels; and Alastair Roberts, who firmly and graciously guided me through writing my first paper on the Sabbath. You were more than teachers to me, and this book is the fruits of your patient mentorship.

I also want to thank the scholars whose work on Leviticus inspired me to read it carefully and imaginatively. Especially Mark Garcia, who suggested reading Leviticus as a metaphysical treatise; Ephraim Radner, who commended theological attention to its relentlessly concrete figures; Victor Austin, who modeled reading the Pentateuch for wisdom and lectured on Leviticus and friendship; and Gary Anderson, who modeled writing about the development of Levitical institutions throughout Christian Scriptures and Jewish liturgical texts. Thank you for pioneering this Levitical path.

I want to thank St. John's Anglican Church in Petaluma for supporting my research and writing with your finances and your prayers, for raising me in the faith, for sponsoring me for ordination, and for buying pizza and scheduling and attending "guest lectures" every time I come home to visit. Thank you, collectively, for calling me to serve the Church with my gifts.

I want to thank all of my students at Maryvale Preparatory Academy in Phoenix, AZ and The Field School in Chicago, IL. You are wise beyond your years, and your questions and insights into the texts we read together in our classrooms, especially the Frederick Douglass speeches I cite in this book, have formed me as a reader, a thinker, and a teacher. I will always be grateful for our time together, and I won't forget you.

I want to thank my academic mentors at Nashotah House Theological Seminary. Especially Travis Bott, who advised the thesis that became the conference paper that became this book; Garwood Anderson, who read my thesis with both a critical and appreciative eye; and Paul Wheatley and Hans Boersma for treating me as much like a colleague as a student. You trained me as a scholar and helped me become a "Master" of Sacred Theology.

I want to thank the team at Athanasius Press. Peter Leithart, again, for approaching me at the end of a conference presentation in July 2021 and asking, "Can you give me 30,000 words on that?" Your enthusiasm for this project has meant the world. John Barach for unimaginably scrupulous attention to theological and editorial content. You bore the responsibility of identifying all contradictions, overstatements, and mis-citations, and allowing me to present a "clean" manuscript to our readers. Ashton Moats for poring over commas, dashes, quotation marks, and abbreviations, and Emma Leithart and Zach Parker, for managing the production of this volume from start to finish. You all took this project over the finish line. Thanks to you, I have finished this book project feeling not exhausted, but refreshed, inspired, and eager to write another one.

Finally, I want to thank two more people who weren't paid by anyone, and who have supported me personally throughout the process. Peter Gross, who read my manuscript, told me it was pandering, and helped me find my voice; and Aleana Saldaña, who only interrupted my writing to remind me to eat and exercise, boasted about me among her friends, and never let me forget the heart which animated my studies. Your support means the world.

INTRODUCTION

> *"Remember the Sabbath, to keep it holy."*
> Exodus 20:8

> *"Proclaim the appointed feasts of Yahweh at the appointed time."*
> Leviticus 23:4

This book is called *Sunday* because, simply put, it is a treatise on the topic of Sunday in Scripture. But before it gets to the New Testament and the particular passages that describe "the first day of the week" or "the Lord's Day," it starts with concepts of liturgical time and liturgical timekeeping instituted in the Old Testament.

It begins with a study of the Sabbath in the Pentateuch—what it means and how it characterizes the rest of Israel's calendar (Chapter 1). Then it offers several theses on the meaning of holidays and history in the Bible (Chapter 2). Those two chapters lay the foundation for three studies of Luke's reception and development of liturgical timekeeping concepts: the Sabbath (Chapter 3), the Passover (Chapter 4), and the Feast of Firstfruits (Chapter 5). A final chapter discusses the ways in which the New Testament presents "the first day of the week" as a genuinely new liturgical institution that draws from these Old Testament traditions, and then suggests some implications for the Church (Chapter 6).

A friend told me once—and I haven't forgotten his words—that the deepest friendships are formed not by sharing the same answers, but by mutual devotion to shared questions. Here, then, as an extension of whatever kind of friendship I may share with my readers, is an introduction to four of the questions that I have asked—and the circumstances that provoked them—that have lent this treatise its particular shape.

A Personal Question

It hit me for the first time in college, when I was invited to two events on the same Tuesday night in mid-December: One was a study session for a fairly consequential final exam, and the other was a Lessons and Carols service at a local Anglican church. Both events sounded important and interesting, and I felt mildly upset at having to choose one over the other. It took me until the next day to understand why.

What I realized was that I had subscribed, unintentionally, not to two discrete events, but to two *communities* governed by two calendars. As a matriculated member of my university, I had taken on my school as *alma mater*, which I learned was Latin for "nourishing mother." As a good kid, I kept Mom's calendar—saving up my stress for the nights before finals week, visiting home at Christmas, and finding seasonal employment for the summers. As a baptized and confirmed Christian, I had taken on the Church as *notre dame*, which I learned was French for "our Lady." As a good kid, I kept *that* mom's calendar, too—resisting the commercialization of Christmas in December to some degree in order to keep a holy Advent.

Neither my school nor my church would have been betrayed by my choice, but that small conflict I felt unlocked for me the fact that most people belong to multiple communities with conflicting calendars and that people who keep time with the same group of people are bonded in certain ways.

I saw medical students finding refuge in each other and

INTRODUCTION

practicing rest during their short breaks between two-week long clinical rotations, my friends who weren't teachers feeling frustrated that they couldn't join the rest of us on our summer vacations, my Native American middle school students missing major school events because they were going back to the Hopi reservation to celebrate a high holiday that their white friends would never quite understand, and my Roman Catholic colleagues using their "religious exemption" to require our public school administrators to hire extra substitute teachers while they took an hour off from work on Ash Wednesday—a "day of holy obligation"—to attend midday mass and receive their ashes.

That set up the first question: *As a member of many bodies—my family, my school, my church, my nation, and Christ Himself—how do I respond to the inner and outer conflicts that I experience when the calendars of those bodies come into competition with one another?*

A Teacher's Question

For several years, I worked as a public school teacher. Our class's discipline was "humane letters," and our subject was America. We read American literature, history, poetry, letters and journals, founding documents, executive orders, and inaugural addresses.

During that time, I thought a lot about the goals of a course in American letters. There was, first of all, the publicly-mandated goal that ELA (English Language Arts) classrooms align their lessons with the mastery of state standards of reading comprehension and writing proficiency.

Alongside these lay other goals for personal formation: cultivating a love for reading, a civility and sincerity in discussion, a setting of the mind on things above, thoughtful consideration of ideas about freedom and authority, justice and peace, the letter and the spirit of the law.

In my reading, I came across an inspiring notion of "citizenship" from Eugen Rosenstock-Huessy that proved fruitful as I continued to organize and lead the course. In one place,

SUNDAY

Rosenstock-Huessy posits that a true "citizen" is one who loves and embodies his *polis*'s ideals in such a way that, were his civilization to die, he could recreate those institutions himself.[1]

A true American, then, for Rosenstock-Huessy, could land on the moon, transcribe large portions of the Declaration and the Constitution from memory, reinstitute a multi-branch governing structure that balanced its powers, populate a balanced court, and train juries. In order to get there, such a student not only would have to memorize key facts and reproduce them on a test, but also would have to wrestle with American ideas and institutions and develop a sense of courage and industry. He'd read Benjamin Franklin's autobiography, Washington's letters, Jefferson's journals, Frederick Douglass's and Abraham Lincoln's speeches, and Ida B. Wells's journalism.

I liked that.

As my students undertook these studies, it became one of my goals to give them a critically appreciative understanding of our institutions—voting, how bills become laws, and our federal holidays.

This raised some lively questions. From the very beginning of our studies, students asked hard questions. One Black student asked, just a couple of weeks in, "How are we supposed to celebrate the Fourth of July if my ancestors weren't declared free until the 1860s?" If this student was going to become a "citizen" in the way Rosenstock-Huessy and I hoped he would, he would need a satisfactory answer to his question.

That question, and others, plunged me into a study of the development of holidays at the state and federal levels, the histories of their celebration, the genre of holiday speeches by significant political figures, and the ideals for which they stand.

One thing I have come to understand about holidays is their inherently *aspirational* quality. The Fourth of July commemorates a real emancipation, but only a partial one—*some* people in *some* ways from *some* powers, with hopes to grow. Scripture bears

---

1. See James Panero, "Hart to Hart," *The New Criterion* (Oct 17, 2006), https://newcriterion.com/blogs/dispatch/hart-to-hart.

INTRODUCTION

witness to this as well: Not even Joshua was able to lead the people into rest, says Hebrews, and there remains for the people of God a future Sabbath.

The United States, Israel, and the Church all value the notion of liberty. We each celebrate it in our holidays, and we each aspire to realize "true freedom"—as we understand it and as it makes sense within our matrices of institutions—that is, within our particular histories.

Our histories are histories of voting rights and taxation, Sabbath-keeping and right worship, ecclesial hierarchy structures and the doctrine of justification. The history of any given body of people is, from one angle, the refining and working out of that body's aspirational ideals.

I learned that Frederick Douglass had raised the very same question as my student in a speech of his own: "What, to the slave, is the Fourth of July?" I also learned that Dietrich Bonhoeffer preached a sermon in 1932 about the theological meaning of Memorial Day during the rise of the National Socialist Party and its charismatic leader, Adolf Hitler: How do we remember World War I with compassion *and* humility, knowing that Christ leads us through death into salvation? There was a whole genre of oratory that consisted of theological and ethical reflection on national holidays.

That is how I got to my second question: *How do I teach canonical history texts in a way that leads youth into sincere, critical, courageous, and creative participation in the United States' civic institutions, including its festal traditions?*

A Ministry Question

In addition to teaching humane letters, I am a clergyman in the Anglican Church whose office it is, among other things, to call Christians to worship and to preside over our liturgical rites, both as preacher and celebrant.

This responsibility, together with my work as a teacher, led me to the figure of Moses, addressed by God in Leviticus 23:4 and

SUNDAY

installed with the responsibility of proclaiming "the appointed feasts of Yahweh ... at the appointed time."

I am not Moses, I am not an Israelite, and I am not an heir of Israel's particular festal tradition. But as a Christian, I am an heir of both testaments, including books like Leviticus that disclose a social imagination for what it means and what it looks like to be God's people in the world. And as a priest, I am charged, in the shadow of Moses, to call God's people to meet Him at the times appointed.

Israel has a rich tradition of relating their history to their institutions. If I had been born 3,000 years ago, I think I would have loved teaching civics in biblical Israel. Genesis 1 explains the Sabbath. Exodus explains most of the rest of the feasts. In my graduate studies, I paid attention to the ways in which Israel related to the *Megillot*, five short books from the "Writings" that were read liturgically during particular feasts: I learned that the Song of Songs was read on the Passover Sabbath, Ruth on the morning of Pentecost, Lamentations on the Ninth of Av, Ecclesiastes on the Sabbath of the Feast of Tabernacles, and Esther on Purim. The Esther connection is obvious. The Song of Songs connection is subtle and tasty: Yahweh is the bridegroom who says, "Come away with me" to the bride who is abused in the streets of her city.

On one level, I was simply envious of the biblical material available to Jewish catechists to invite their youth into sincere, critical, courageous, and creative participation in their body's institutions and festal traditions. I wished that the church I belonged to related entire books of the Bible to our holidays.

"Sunday," also called "the Lord's Day," is a Christian institution. It is related to a moment in our history, the significance of which cannot be overstated: the resurrection of Jesus Christ. And so when a pastor—or priest, or elder, or celebrant—stands before a Christian congregation on a Sunday morning, that person participates in a kind of work analogous to the kind of work I found myself doing in my public school classroom: leading members of

INTRODUCTION

a particular body into sincere, critical, courageous, and creative participation in its institutions—including its festal traditions.

Yahweh's instructions to Moses in Leviticus 23:4 to "proclaim the appointed feasts of Yahweh ... at the appointed time" are passed on to the Christian pastor, and we owe it to the Lord to fulfill that charge in the Spirit of Jesus. That's the first part of the question: *How, then, do I fulfill Yahweh's instructions to Moses in the Spirit of Jesus?* Then, more specifically, I asked, *How do I call God's people to keep the command, "Remember the Sabbath," in the Spirit of Jesus?*

A Research Question

The more I read about liturgical historiography in the Old Testament, the more I became curious about liturgical historiography in the *New* Testament. I noted that Luke had written the most history, so he made me the most curious. He was also the only New Testament historian to tell, not one, but *two* stories that begin with the phrase, "on the first day of the week."

That was the beginning of my official research question: *How does Luke use the Old Testament's liturgical institutions to frame new histories for the Church?*

My answer to that question, in short, is that one of the accomplishments of Luke's history is his major contribution to the configuration of the Christian Sunday, a new liturgical concept for the new covenant, depicted as a combination of the Sabbath, of Passover, and of Firstfruits.

What follows in these chapters is a proposal for how to keep Yahweh's commands to proclaim the appointed feasts at the appointed time (Lev 23:4) and to remember the Sabbath (Exod 20:8); and, in essence, a biblical answer to the question, *What does Sunday mean?*

1 BIG SABBATH

"The Sabbath was made for man."
Mark 2:27

"The Sabbaths are our great cathedrals."
Abraham Joshua Heschel

We can't think well about Christian time, and especially not the concept of Sunday, without thinking deeply about the Sabbath. This chapter is a reflection on the meaning of the Sabbath as it is disclosed in the first three books of the Bible.

The Sabbath is a holy day, the seventh day of the week, set apart by Yahweh from the very beginning as a day of rest. It is introduced at the beginning of Genesis, makes a dramatic appearance midway through Exodus, and then flames out in kaleidoscopic glory at the end of Leviticus. The Sabbath is a "day," but it's not *just* a day; and it's definitely about "rest," but it's not *just* about rest.

The Christian Sunday is not a carbon copy of Israel's Sabbath, but it bears a striking resemblance to it, and we simply cannot understand Sunday until we have understood the Sabbath. That's part of what Paul means when he says that Israel's festivals and Sabbaths "are a shadow of the things to come," while "the substance belongs to Christ" (Col 2:16–17). And that's also at least part of what John means when he calls Sunday "the Lord's Day" (Rev 1:10).

God in the Garden

We see a Sabbath at the very beginning of the Bible. After creating a world in six days, God marks off the "week" as a unit of time by resting on the seventh day. The words are simple, and their meaning sits on the surface of the text:

> Thus the heavens and the earth were finished, and all the host of them. And on the seventh day God finished his work that he had done, and he rested on the seventh day from all his work that he had done. So God blessed the seventh day and made it holy, because on it God rested from all his work that he had done in creation. (Gen 2:1–3)

Reflecting on the key words takes readers most of the way there: *finished*, *work*, *seventh day*, and *rest*.

The same meaning is also tucked just beneath the surface. In the original language, this short passage is made up of thirty-five words distributed into five clauses for an average of seven words per clause. The first clause is short, and the fifth clause is long, but the middle three clauses each contain seven words, signifying their importance. Each of those seven-word clauses includes the words, "the seventh day." Look at them:

> "And on the seventh day God finished his work that he had done" (2:2a).
>
> "And he rested on *the seventh day* from all his work that he had done" (2:2b).
>
> "So God blessed *the seventh day* and made it holy ..." (2:3a).

The "sevenly" (that's my new word—it rhymes with "heavenly," and I'm trying to make it happen) shape of the passage doesn't give us any new information, but it reinforces that *the text really means what it says*. It matters that it's the seventh day; it matters that God *finishes* and *blesses*, and that the verb at the center of the structure is *rest*; and it matters that Israel's Sabbath is a participation in *God's* finishing, blessing, and resting.

In the next book, Exodus, Yahweh will sometimes call the Sabbath "*the* Sabbath," but He also coins the phrase "*my* Sabbaths." As in, "Above all you shall keep *my* Sabbaths ... that you may know that I, Yahweh, sanctify you" (31:13). One of Yahweh's big talking points is that Israel is *His* creation. When He tells them about His plans for them, He often reminds them that it stands to reason, then, that because He is their Creator, He will also *finish* His work of creating them, *bless* them, and *rest* among them. All of Yahweh's future work is foreshadowed and crystallized in Genesis 2:1–3: *Yahweh is our Creator, and not we ourselves. He blesses us, finishes the work He began in us, and rests among us.* And so the main point of the Sabbath is not simply to keep "the" Sabbath or "a" Sabbath in general, but to keep the Sabbath *of* Yahweh *with* Yahweh.

But that's getting too theological too quickly.

It's worth pausing here and acknowledging that in the Church, our constructive thinking about the Sabbath doesn't often make it past Genesis. "God in the Garden" is the main Old Testament Sabbath story we know. And so we read Genesis 2:1–3, close our Bibles, close our eyes, and try to be like God. Here's how that tired sermon goes: *Church, if only we could, like God, in the "gardens" of our own lives, take some time off and learn how to rest, we will be doing what we see our Father doing* (John 5:19).

This understanding of rest works great if you live by yourself in a garden—and you don't have kids, or you're one of the many people whose workplaces require them to work on Sundays. But this understanding of rest is also the fantasy of the Main Villain in the Bible's next book.

Pharaoh Takes on the Lord of the Sabbath

Read Genesis quickly, and you won't see the Sabbath featured again. It's not an explicit part of Abraham's life, or of Isaac's or Jacob's or Joseph's, for that matter. In fact, it won't come up again until after Israel's exodus from Egypt. When it does resurface, it comes in the form of a command in Exodus 16 and then as one of "The Ten" in Exodus 20.

Most of "The Ten" are short. Three of the commands are one word long; one is four words; four more run between thirteen and fifteen words each; but the Sabbath Command weighs in at fifty-six words, nearly as many words as eight of the other commands combined. The fact that it is so wordy doesn't tell us exactly what the command means, but it suggests that there is a reason that when Moses sent it to his publisher, they decided not to cut any of his words. Yahweh isn't one to add fluff to meet word count, especially not in a passage like "The Ten Words" (Exod 20:1–20), which is famous for its brevity, so the reader ought to be suspicious that every detail matters, both to Moses and to God. Here is the command in full:

> Remember the Sabbath day, to keep it holy. Six days you shall labor, and do all your work, but the seventh day is a Sabbath to Yahweh your God. On it you shall not do any work, you, or your son, or your daughter, your male servant, or your female servant, or your livestock, or the sojourner who is within your gates. For in six days Yahweh made heaven and earth, the sea, and all that is in them, and rested on the seventh day. Therefore Yahweh blessed the Sabbath day and made it holy. (Exod 20:8–11)

Some of the words and phrases in this passage are identical to those in Genesis: The Sabbath is still the seventh day, it still involves not working, and its meaning still has to do with the fact that Yahweh rested on and blessed the seventh day. But this command hits differently when you hear it in the key of Exodus, which is the story of Yahweh upstaging Pharaoh and bringing His people out to form them into a new, anti-Pharaonic nation. In the key of Exodus, the Sabbath is just as much about Pharaoh as it is about Israel.

In a manner of speaking, Exodus depicts Pharaoh as a frustrated demigod trying to recreate Genesis 1. Only he has some crippling limitations. Yahweh is unlike other gods, in that He

SUNDAY

creates everything out of nothing. The Bible tells us that God the Father creates all things *through* and *in* God the Son; that He creates them by the power of God the Holy Spirit; and that He creates in the joyful company of His ministering spirits, the angels. With such a great crew, Yahweh finishes His world in six days and then sets the seventh day apart by resting on it. Yahweh's rest does not come at the expense of any other agent, divine or otherwise. The Father rests together with His Son and His Spirit. Presumably, His heavenly hosts rest, and the land itself rests.

There isn't some cohort of underpaid Quality Assurance spirits or contracted Post-Production angels putting finishing touches on the pine trees or updating the badgers' central nervous system after 5:00 pm on a Friday. When Yahweh clocks out, everyone rests.

Genesis 1 is an impossible act to follow, but that doesn't stop Pharaoh the Fool from trying.

Pharaoh was building a world, too, called Egypt, and the story of Exodus starts when the Israelites were tasked with building storage cities, namely Pithom and Raamses (Exod 1:14). In the four verses that describe the Israelites' work, the text belabors the point that Egypt made Israel work (*'abad*) as slaves, making their lives bitter with hard service (*'abōd*), in mortar and brick and all kinds of work (*'abōd*) in the field, in all the work (*'abōd*) they made them do.

An *abad* job is *a bad* job.[1] Of all the Hebrew words that mean "work," this one denotes servile work and forced labor, and the word "slave" (*ebed*) is simply the noun version of the same word.

Moses and Aaron ask Pharaoh for three days' leave to worship Yahweh in the wilderness, and he scoffs, "you make them rest (*shabat*) from their burdens!" (5:4). Pharaoh says this because of a problem he is facing: The Israelites are breeding and growing strong, and he knows that releasing them unto rest will only make them stronger.

According to the human resources textbooks I read as an

---

1. In Exodus, that is. The term takes on a different meaning in Leviticus, when it refers to the "new" work of the priests.

undergraduate business major, executives should *want* a strong and well-rested workforce. But not when it's *abad* work. In any case, Pharaoh's decision not to rest the Israelites doesn't work, and he fails to accomplish in his own lifetime what Yahweh achieved in six days.

The first lesson here is that if you're going to hire a general contractor and pay them for time and materials, don't hire Pharaoh. The second lesson is that when Yahweh says, "Do no work" in the Sabbath Command, He is not discussing work as an abstract notion. He is discussing the particular work of world-building: the work He did in Genesis 1–2, and the work that Pharaoh made the Israelites do in Egypt. That's why it matters that the Sabbath is not a command given to Israel in general, but to the foremen of new worlds, big and small; a command given to Pharaohs, bishops, plant managers, teachers, and heads of multi-family households in agrarian economies.

The world rested in Genesis when Yahweh rested. Pharaoh wouldn't rest, and neither could any of his workforce.

The letter of the law starts with the part we already know from Genesis: "You shall not do any work." But it continues with a specific and thorough list: "you, or your son, or your daughter, your male servant, or your female servant, or your livestock, or the sojourner who is within your gates."

This means that, in the key of Exodus, keeping the Sabbath means two things. First, it means that world-builders and foremen should rest on the seventh day; that is, they should do no work themselves. But it also means keeping the members of their household from doing the work that they employ them to do. In this way, the Sabbath applies to Pharaoh before it applies to Israel. It's not Israel's fault that they had to work Saturday shifts in Egypt. The archetypal story about someone being put to death for breaking the Sabbath is not the one about the man gathering sticks (Num 15:32–36), but the story of Pharaoh refusing to let his servants go. He may have been reclining under the palms with a cold stein of premodern beer—*doing no work*—but he neglected the weightier matters of the Sabbath law—justice and mercy and

SUNDAY

faith. And the wages of this sin of his were the death of his firstborn, the destruction of his empire, and his own death in the Sea.

I have imagined Pharaoh lounging poolside—palms waving, sunglasses on, and a committee of priests playing music somewhere behind him. They're playing "instrumental-relaxing" songs because Pharaoh takes Saturdays off for self-care. His buddy who works at Papyrus Press sent him a review copy of a new book of personal devotions called *Firm Faith for Pharaohs*, and he's on the chapter called "Being Like God: Sabbath-Keeping for Emperors in the Ancient Near East." He reads the stirring story of God resting in the Garden and resolves quietly to himself, *This building campaign is so stressful, and my phone has been ringing off the hook with issues from foremen. One of them just got killed by a runaway Israelite. I'm going to keep a rigid discipline of resting on the seventh day, just like God. I'm going to turn my phone off, get a deep tissue massage, and only eat food that's been prepared by my servants.* Content with this "personal application" and negligent of all of the men and women upon whose active and compulsory labor his rest depends, Pharaoh shuts his eyes and frowns, trying to tune out the conversation his advisors are having about shocking reports of fish dying in the Nile.

Reading the Sabbath in the key of Exodus clarifies that the Sabbath isn't merely about people "in general" resting from work "in general." Exodus depicts a world in which Yahweh isn't the only world-building god and, for gods like Pharaoh, ambitions depend on the subjugation of those who work with their actual hands. Placing this command *right after* Israel's Exodus and *right before* the construction of the tabernacle and the journey to Canaan sends both a clear promise and a warning. The clear promise is that Yahweh sees the suffering of laborers, and that He will hold their employers accountable. The warning is that Israel learned management from Pharaoh and his foremen, and they're in danger of acting more like Egyptians than like Yahweh.

Aren't we all?

That's why Yahweh's Sabbaths matter so much. And why the first word in the command is "Remember," and not "Keep."

1 BIG SABBATH

The Sabbath is a history lesson and Israel's first national holiday, even before the Passover. Every week, Israel corporately *remembers* that Yahweh brought them out of Pharaoh's house of slavery and is creating a new nation out of them. But remembering the Sabbath doesn't just mean retelling or reimagining the exodus; it means *reenacting* it. Every seventh day, every Foreman Figure in Israel is required by law to let their people go. By participating in these regular, legislated, peaceful reenactments of the Exodus, Israel celebrates their national history and sanctifies themselves as Yahweh's nation. They refine their notions of freedom and equity, as well as the meaning of the dogma that Yahweh alone is their Creator. Yahweh the World-Builder keeps the same Sabbath He commands. This is why He says, "*Above all* you shall keep my Sabbaths" (Exod 31:13).

But while He still has them at Sinai, Yahweh has a lot more to say about the Sabbath. The Sabbath isn't just one law out of Ten. In fact, He's going to use it as the foundation for two more kinds of laws: His Manumission Laws (Exod 21:2–6; Deut 15:12–15) and His Calendar (Lev 23, 25).

The Manumission Laws

Turn the page from Exodus 20 to Exodus 21, and the very first non-Ten-Commandment commandment is a Manumission Law based on the Sabbath (21:2–6).

First, some ideological context: The books of the Law imagine an economic system in which each tribe, and then each family within each tribe, settles and develops fixed plots of land. For those who would like to expand their allotments, Joshua does not direct them to buy each other out but to expand their borders by conquering new territory. They'll continue to keep animals, but now they'll grow crops: That's the privilege and the right of a non-wandering people. Both their food and their religious offerings will come from the fruitfulness and multiplication of their seed-bearing plants and their seed-bearing animals. Naturally, the task of "managing" the household will fall to some—to keep the scheme simple, I'll continue to call these managers

SUNDAY

"Foreman Figures"—and the more laborious work will fall to the children, the servants, and the livestock. This is why the Sabbath Command is addressed to "you, or your son, or your daughter, your male servant, or your female servant, or your livestock."

If, however, for whatever reason, a man fails to run a profitable household—his crop fails or his health declines, he needs to pay a debt or make restitution for a property crime—he may voluntarily enter a contract of service with a healthier or more prudent landowner as a "servant." This is the context of the Manumission Law.

For such a man, his contract of service expires *in the seventh year*, at which time he shall "go out free, for nothing" (Exod 21:2), and, if he enters his term of service as a married man, he is permitted to take his wife with him when he goes.

A little bit of math fleshes out how the Sabbath applies to this man. Given that Israel kept a twelve month calendar that matched the lunar cycles and that they divided their months into four weeks and that this contract of service lasted, at most, six years, when a man entered himself or another member of his family into contractual servitude to a landowning neighbor, he knew exactly what he was signing them up for: no more than 288 weeks of labor on another family's property, including the weekly cadence of the Sabbath, which reminded both him and his owner of their co-dignity and co-equal membership in Yahweh's new nation. After 288 weeks of humane servitude and 288 Sabbaths, he could expect to be released and restored to his own property.

That's the Manumission Law of Exodus 21.

Deuteronomy 15:12–15 elaborates on this law. Called by some scholars an "update" to Exodus 21:2–6, the Deuteronomy version not only describes *when* a slave was set to be released but also stipulates *how*:

> And when you let him go free from you, you shall not let him go empty-handed. You shall furnish him liberally out of your flock, out of your threshing floor, and out of your winepress. As Yahweh your God has blessed you, you shall give to him. You shall remember that you were a slave in the land of Egypt.

1 BIG SABBATH

Pharaoh wanted to keep his male and female slaves indefinitely, but Yahweh forced him to let them go. He also squeezed Egypt into giving Israel "articles of silver and articles of gold"—the materials they would use to build the tabernacle. And so, even if a Foreman Figure in Israel might have *wanted* to hold onto his slaves for longer than six years, Yahweh's Law made similar requirements. They'd have to voluntarily manumit their slaves, and then, since no one would need gold once the tabernacle was built, they had to give them the physical capital—livestock, grain, and wine—that they would need to bring offerings to the tabernacle and establish a livelihood at home. Like the Sabbath (Exod 20:8–11), the Manumission Law (Exod 21:2–6; Deut 15:12–15) is another law with the subtext, "Yahweh's nation is not like Pharaoh's nation."

Before this was a law, it was simply the story of Jacob and Laban (Gen 29–31). After having been sent away by his father, Isaac, Jacob meets some men from Haran who bring him to meet his uncle, Laban. Laban receives Jacob like a son, and he insists that Jacob not work "for nothing" (29:15). So Jacob asks for Rachel, works seven years for her, and ends up being tricked into marrying Leah. He works seven more years for Rachel and, because of his love for her, the years fly by. After entering a third contract for six more years of work—twenty total—God helps him leave Laban with both of his wives and with all of the livestock that he won by his trickery.

Israel's Manumission Law commemorates the story of Jacob and Laban, and it reminds Israel that Yahweh's laws protect at least one kind of poor: those who, like Jacob, must, for a time, earn a living by laboring on and building up another man's land. Like so many of us.

The Sabbath doesn't just mean releasing slaves on the seventh day; it means restoring Jacob and all of his sons to fruitful life on their own land in the seventh year. Yahweh's Sabbath is even more than a one-day-a-week observance, a way of telling history, and Israel's first national holiday; it's also a relentlessly concrete picture of what it means to "Love your neighbor as yourself," and it's a crystallization of the Pentateuch's economic vision.

Yahweh's Sevenly Calendar

In Leviticus 23, Yahweh gives Israel an entire calendar of feasts all at once. The significance of receiving a full calendar of feasts, all at once, is easier to understand when we consider it in contrast to the United States' calendar of federal holidays.

The United States' Calendar

In 1870, on behalf of the United States government, Ulysses S. Grant declared the first four federal holidays, all of which were already being widely observed at state and local levels: New Year's Day on January 1st, Independence Day on July 4th, Thanksgiving Day on the fourth-ish Thursday of November, and Christmas on December 25th. What's funny to me about this is how these holidays have almost nothing in common.

The history of January 1st dates all the way back to the reign of Julius Caesar. As the story goes, Roman politicians had been abusing the lunar calendar for centuries—adding or subtracting days in order to serve their political ends. So Julius Caesar hired the Greek astronomer, Sosogines, who pushed Rome to adopt a solar calendar, like the Egyptians. He went for it, adding sixty-seven days to the year we call 46 BC, making the first day of the month of Janus the first day of the year, according to the new "Julian calendar."

Having two faces, Janus could simultaneously look back into the previous year and forward into the new one. Following Caesar's assassination, Mark Antony changed the name of one of the other months from "Quintilius" to "Julius," also known as "July." By declaring January 1st a federal holiday, President Grant did nothing more than affirm his nation's subscription to and orientation around the Julian calendar. America observes the day, and the Big Ball in New York has become a cultural icon, but it's not exactly what we might call an "American holiday."

1 BIG SABBATH

The Fourth of July is a truly American holiday, rooted not in Roman politics but in our founding narrative. It was on July 2, 1776, that the delegates of the Second Continental Congress voted to approve Richard Henry Lee's resolution to legally separate from Great Britain. The next day, July 3rd, John Adams wrote to his wife, Abigail, the following prediction:

> The second day of July 1776, will be the most memorable epoch in the history of America. I am apt to believe that it will be celebrated by succeeding generations as the great anniversary festival. It ought to be commemorated as the day of deliverance, by solemn acts of devotion to God Almighty. It ought to be solemnized with pomp and parade, with shows, games, sports, guns, bells, bonfires, and illuminations, from one end of this continent to the other, from this time forward forever more.[2]

He was close. It wasn't until the next day, July 4th, that the Congress voted to approve the Declaration of Independence, authored by the Committee of Five, and chiefly by Thomas Jefferson. This anniversary was celebrated the next year on July 4th and, in 1781, the Massachusetts state legislature became the first to legally recognize it as a "day of deliverance." Although the anniversary was observed in various ways in most states, it wouldn't be recognized as a federal holiday until Congress passed Senator Hannibal Hamlin's (D-ME) bill in 1870, when private companies had scheduled major public groundbreaking ceremonies that day for construction on the Erie Canal and the Baltimore and Ohio Railroad, and some of Congress didn't want *this* celebration to overshadow the celebration of national independence. It wouldn't become a *paid* federal holiday until Congress passed a joint resolution (HJ resolution No. 551; pub. res. no. 127) to that effect in 1938. That's a lot like the difference between the Manumission Laws of Exodus 21:2–6 and then Deuteronomy 15:12–15. First, release without pay; then, release plus provisions.

Ain't that just the way?

It's hard to say exactly when the first Thanksgiving was and,

---

2. From a letter from John Adams to Abigail Adams, July 3, 1776.

for many, the way we tell its origin story is itself morally charged. That shouldn't be surprising because origin stories under the sun are inherently contentious. Americans who move to England talk about the awkwardness of celebrating the Fourth of July over there. It's not difficult to imagine the internal struggle of an Egyptian expat being told to keep Yahweh's Sabbaths if they wanted to be included in His covenant community (i.e. "the foreigner who keeps my Sabbaths," Isa 56) under His covenant sign (Exod 31:13).

Whatever its mythic origins, the *federal* holiday we call Thanksgiving didn't take place until the states established a federal government. It was within the first year of George Washington's presidency when he issued an executive proclamation, calling Thursday, November 26, 1789, a "day of national thanksgiving and prayer." Prior to that day, many (religious) colonists had a lively practice of identifying and setting aside occasional days for fasting and thanksgiving. After the British General, John Burgoyne, waved the white flag at Saratoga in October 1777, the Continental Congress proposed setting aside a national day to recognize the victory. As Commander of the Continental Army, the responsibility fell to General George Washington, who agreed, naming December 18, 1777 as the first national thanksgiving day—a day that had nothing to do with pilgrims or native nations or corn on the cob. In 1789, Representative Elias Boudinot (NJ) requested that Congress ask now-President George Washington to declare another national thanksgiving, this one in response to the creation of the new federal Constitution. Washington agreed, and that was the 1789 one. He wouldn't call another one until six years later, and he called that one in February.

Presidents continued to call national thanksgivings until 1863, when Abraham Lincoln famously articulated the meaning of the holiday and fixed a time: He called his "fellow-citizens in every part of the United States, and also those who are at sea and those who are sojourning in foreign lands, to set apart and observe the last Thursday of November next as a day of thanksgiving and praise for our beneficent Father who dwelleth in the heavens."

This "last Thursday" date stuck until 1939, when Franklin

Delano Roosevelt, in an attempt to stimulate a depressed economy, moved Thanksgiving one week earlier in order to extend the season of Christmas shopping by seven days. Congress protested unsuccessfully, and the economists I've read don't believe Roosevelt's revision accomplished very much. His gimmick failed again in 1940, and so, in 1941 he repented, and the dispute was settled by the signing of a joint resolution to fix the date on the fourth Thursday of November, a compromise between the "last Thursday" and the "next to last." His intention was to "stabilize the date so that there be no confusion at any time in the future." And that settled that.

I say all this to point out, by way of contrast to Israel's calendar, that the United States' first federal holidays are a patchwork. There is Caesar's politically useful nod to Janus, the two-faced Roman god. Then there's the commemoration of the Continental Congress's vote to approve and sign the Committee of Five's final draft of the Declaration of Independence. Then, a national Thanksgiving, first for the creation of the Constitution, and later for God's providence in general. Finally, there's Christmas, which we often forget is not only a religious holiday but also a federal one.

Yahweh's Calendar

Yahweh's calendar is a coherent whole, designed by Himself and announced all at once to Moses. In Leviticus 23, Yahweh comes out with strong instructions for His president: "These are the appointed feasts of Yahweh *that you shall proclaim* as holy convocation; *they are my appointed feasts*" (Lev 23:2). Yahweh's chief feasts were not created by Congress or amended by presidents. Yahweh declares them, and Moses proclaims them.[3]

Yahweh's calendar begins with the Sabbath (23:3), and then His other festivals are all meaningfully related to the Sabbath. For one, the other six feasts contain explicit instructions to "do no work" (23:7–8, 25, 28, 30–31, 35–36). That means that, unlike the

---

3. Mordecai adds Purim (Esth 9:20–32), but this is an exception. I will say more about Esther in later chapters.

SUNDAY

United States' festal calendar, which has no coherence, Yahweh establishes "the Sabbath" as Israel's festal principle.[4]

But the relationship is also just beneath the surface. There are seven ways in which Yahweh bases His appointed feasts on the number "seven":

One, every seventh day is a Sabbath.

Two, Yahweh's annual calendar (Lev 23) consists of descriptions of seven festal times: the Sabbath (23:3), Passover (23:4–8), Firstfruits (23:9–14), Weeks / Pentecost (23:15–22), Trumpets (23:23–25), the Day of Coverings / Atonement (23:26–32), and Booths / Tabernacles (23:33–43).

Three, every seventh *year* is a Sabbath Year of rest for the parts of the land that bear crops: "seventh day" for persons and animals, "seventh year" for the land. Legislation for the Sabbath Year repeats the same cast of characters as in the legislation for the Sabbath Day law (Exod 20:8–11) and tells them how they will eat together: "The Sabbath of the land shall provide food for you, for yourself and for your male and female slaves and for your hired servant and the sojourner who lives with you, and for your cattle and for the wild animals that are in your land: all its yield shall be for food" (Lev 25:6–7).

The Sabbath Year is more than a break for the land. If the land can't work, then neither landowners nor day laborers have any work to do. The Sabbath Year is a regular return to the conditions of the Garden of Eden for those who learned the slave economy in Egypt. Just as in Eden, every seventh year there is "no man to cultivate the ground" (Gen 2:5). In our day and age, some kinds of workers—some pastors, professors—have the opportunity for paid sabbaticals, where they can spend time with their families and work on whatever they didn't have time for in the previous few years. In Israel, everyone gets a Sabbatical that simulates Eden, and it's supposed to help them to emerge like new creations. Each of them—landowner, son, daughter, foreign or

---

4. For a strong discussion of the concept of a "festal principle," see Josef Pieper, *In Tune with the World: A Theory of Festivity* (South Bend, IN: St. Augustine's Press, 1999).

1 BIG SABBATH

domestic slave, animal—is not fundamentally *from Egypt* but *from the Garden*. They are sons of Yahweh and of Adam, not sons of Pharaoh. (Imagine a world where everyone knew this.)

Four, after every seven sevens of years, the president is to proclaim the fiftieth year a Year of Jubilee.[5]

It was common for Mesopotamian kings to begin their new reign with some "edict of liberty" and then give surprise "remissions of debt" as they saw fit. As of the time of writing, United States presidents are trying to cancel certain kinds of student loan debt for certain kinds of students in certain situations while the courts challenge its constitutionality.

Yahweh distinguishes Israel by *scheduling* jubilees. Liberty, remission, and restoration don't depend on the strategies of kings but the fixed rhythms of Yahweh and the obedience of His presidents.

The Jubilee (Lev 25:23–55), which I also like to call the Big Sabbath, has two legal components: the restoration of property (23:23–34) and the restoration of persons (23:35–55). The fundamental principle behind property restoration is that Yahweh owns the land and that, although each family is allotted a tract, they are to consider themselves not land-lords but tenants-in-chief. Every Israelite is to respect the property lines drawn by God and delivered through Moses (Num 33:50–56) and Joshua (Josh 14–19). If a family wished to *expand* their allotment, they were invited to cultivate wild land. The only reason two families would *exchange* land would be the temporary inability of the one family to "make a living" off of their own land and their corresponding need to fall in with another family for a time. When the trumpet sounded on the Day of Atonement in the Jubilee Year, all of the land in rural places and "unwalled" cities was to be released back to its allotted owners, whom Yahweh simply calls His chief tenants.

There are a number of reasons why a person might need to leave his own land to work for a neighbor. A man's family property

---

5. This account of the Year of Jubilee summarizes Michael LeFebvre's work in "Theology and Economics in the Biblical Year of Jubilee," *Bulletin of Evangelical Theology* 2.1 (2015): 31–51.

SUNDAY

may have been sold off, and he may no longer have a way to provide for his family. In this case, the broader family, or clan, should provide him with an opportunity to work *near* home, purchase food at cost, and receive loans without interest. The emphasis of this local welfare program is on keeping a poor brother among his family and near his land. Every seven sevens of years, Israel was refreshed, or new-created. Sons and daughters of slavery were restored as Adams and Eves on well-rested land with well-rested animals. The shadow of Pharaoh and the memory of Egypt loomed large, and Yahweh knew that a nation called to love their neighbors would need to rehearse their economic identities weekly, every seven years, and generationally.

Five, the Feast of Unleavened Bread and the Feast of Tabernacles, the only two feasts spanning more than one day, are each celebrated for seven days. Unleavened Bread starts on the fifteenth day of the first month; Tabernacles starts on the fifteenth day of the seventh month. As Moses Maimonides put it, Unleavened Bread commemorates God's miracles in Egypt, and Tabernacles commemorates God's miracles when they "dwelt in tabernacles" in the wilderness (Lev 23:43).[6]

If Israel had simply declared their independence from Great Britain, they might have gotten away with a one-day celebration and a quick return to work. But they were brought out by Yahweh, who has a habit of taking seven days to do things—not because He is slow, but because He likes the number seven. The *Shemot Rabbah* explains that the Jews were pursued by the Egyptians for seven days before the parting of the Red Sea. Within just a few generations, some Israelites would be living in impressive and relatively comfortable houses, eating well and plentifully off the fat of the land. Their two "independence week" celebrations consisted of annual returns to cheap pantry bread and homemade tents, humble reminders that Yahweh created them from scratch and not they, themselves.

Six, just as the Jubilee is celebrated every seven sevens of

---

6. Moses Maimonides, *The Guide for the Perplexed* (New York: Dover Publications, 2000), III.43.

1 BIG SABBATH

years, Pentecost is celebrated seven sevens of days, plus one, after Firstfruits. Yahweh tells them to count both times: "You shall count seven full weeks" (23:15) and "You shall count seven weeks of years" (25:8). The Sabbath Day was supposed to prepare Israel for the Sabbath Year, which would prepare Israel again for the Big Sabbath, the Jubilee, which completes the Sabbath Vision. Firstfruits was a minor, domestic harvest festival that kicked off the countdown to Pentecost, Israel's major harvest festival. There is a reason why, "When the day of Pentecost arrived, [the disciples] were all together in one place" and that "there were dwelling in Jerusalem Jews, devout men from every nation" (Acts 2:1, 5). In America, kids count down the days to Christmas. They had countdowns to big festivals in Israel, too, but those countdowns were seven sevens of days long.

Seven, the seventh month of the year, Tishri, contains the largest number of Israel's feasts: the Feast of Trumpets, the Day of Atonement, and the Feast of Tabernacles. When we in America talk about "the holidays," we usually mean the stretch from Thanksgiving to Christmas, marked with seeing family, taking time off, engaging in commercial activity, and surrounding ourselves with decorations. Unless you're in school, "the holidays" are the end of the year. When Israel talked about cashing in some of their PTO to leave the city and head home for "the holidays," they're likely to have been talking about the seventh month.

The Sabbath is a Big Deal, and it means a lot of things: The Sabbath is Yahweh's hallowing of the seventh day, and it's the people's weekly commemoration of Yahweh's great works of creation and new creation. The Sabbath is also the legislative principle for releasing sons, slaves, animals, and land to rest every week and again every seven years. It's also a semicentennial reset whose purpose is to prevent generational poverty; it's the sevenly calendar of holidays; and it's Israel's normative approach to telling and remembering and reenacting their history of deliverance.

With all of this in view, who can be surprised when Jesus says that "the Sabbath was made for man" (Mark 2:27)? The Sabbath was made for man from the beginning, and it was immediately developed into a legal institution that provided especially for the poor and instituted a means of loving one's neighbor as oneself. Keeping the Sabbath does not mean, as Jesus reminded the Pharisees, scrupulously abstaining from kinetic activity. It means rejecting Pharaoh and entrusting Yahweh to create, bless, and finish a just and peaceable nation that runs like a city and smells like Eden.

2 YOUR HOLIDAYS

*"Your new moons and your appointed feasts
my soul hates."*
Isaiah 1:14

*"What have I, or those I represent, to do with your
national independence?"*
Frederick Douglass

In the first chapter, I selected and reflected on a handful of passages from the first three books of the Bible, founding books, and sketched out the shape of Israel's Sabbath, which Jesus said was "made for man" (Mark 2:27). What is more difficult to do is to figure out *how* the rest of the Bible—history, prophets, New Testament—receives and develops the Sabbath and other figures of liturgical time, like the Passover, Firstfruits, and the new unit of liturgical time introduced in the New Testament: Sunday.

Disciplined readers of the Bible know that Jesus "fulfills" the Law and that the Law includes the Sabbath. One of my intentions in beginning with a chapter on the Sabbath is to demonstrate how difficult a Law the Sabbath is to identify.

Is it a moral law? Yes.

A ceremonial law? Also, yes.

A judicial law? Yes again.

Does Jesus fulfill the Sabbath Law by *simplifying* its demands, *intensifying* them, or *metaphorizing* them? Hm.

It is certainly a Law, but it's a unique one. It is a law and a covenant sign and a feast. According to some heirs of and commentators upon the Sabbath tradition, it is even a sacred "space." First, Jan Assmann:

> Of all the Ten Commandments, the Sabbath commandment exerted the most far-reaching influence on Judaism during the crucial formative years of exile and the postexilic years in Judea. "It is difficult to find another example," Benno Jacob writes, "where a single and so simple rule, in the absence of all secular compulsion, has so profoundly and lastingly influenced the education of a people.... It [the Sabbath] has been preserved, under the most trying circumstances imaginable, as the purest, most secure and most enduring vessel for monotheism, the one least susceptible to contamination by gentile ideas and customs. In short, it has been largely responsible for helping the people of Israel weather the storms of history." "If Heine was to call the Torah the 'portable fatherland' of Judaism," remarks Alexandra Grund, "then the Sabbath has been a kind of 'portable temple' since the very beginning."[1]

Abraham Heschel says something similar in his famous book about the Sabbath:

> Judaism is a religion of time aiming at the sanctification of time.... Judaism teaches us to be attached to holiness in time, to be attached to sacred events, to learn how to consecrate sanctuaries that emerge from the magnificent stream of a year. The Sabbaths are our great cathedrals.[2]

---

1. Jan Assmann, *The Invention of Religion: Faith and Covenant in the Book of Exodus* (Princeton: Princeton University Press, 2018), 222–23.

2. Abraham Heschel, *The Sabbath: Its Meaning for Modern Man* (New York: H. Wolff, 1951), 8.

2 YOUR HOLIDAYS

Having brought to mind, I hope, the *grandeur* of the Sabbath, I want to argue next that we cannot use stand-alone clobber verses to characterize Jesus' fulfillment of the Sabbath.

One clobber verse "against" the Sabbath comes from Hosea: "I will put an end to all ... her Sabbaths" (2:11). But Jesus says that the Sabbath was made for man. Is it really the mission of the Jesus of the New Testament to carry out this promise from Yahweh, destroying the Sabbath?

Another clobber verse comes from the letter to the Hebrews: "There remains a Sabbath rest for the people of God" (4:9). The letter points to the past, emphasizing what Joshua did not accomplish, and it points to the future, emphasizing what remains for the Christian. But it doesn't say very much about what liturgical time means now. Using this verse to characterize the Sabbath allows us to speak ambiguously about the Sabbath and to defer much of its meaning to an unrealized future. If the "true" Sabbath lies in an unrealized future, what does the Sabbath mean now?

This chapter offers four theses on how the Bible receives and develops the categories of liturgical time introduced in the first three books. As it does, it will continue to reflect on holidays in the American tradition, leaning on several prominent voices from the American festal tradition, and especially on Frederick Douglass, for reasons that will become clearer as the chapter goes on. Throughout these chapters, and more succinctly in a final chapter, I will offer a series of conclusions about what Sunday means in the New Testament and what it means to preside over this weekly commemoration within the historical community that keeps the Sunday feast.

On Critical Words in the Old Testament

The first thesis is a negative one: *The Old Testament's critical words about Israel's feasts, including its words about the Sabbath, are* not *aimed at dismantling the concept of the Sabbath or replacing it with something else.*

Taken together, Genesis, Exodus, and Leviticus disclose an unequivocally positive picture of the Sabbath.

SUNDAY

The Prophets don't.

Here is how Isaiah begins: "New moon and Sabbath and the calling of convocations—I cannot endure iniquity and solemn assembly. Your new moons and your appointed feasts my soul hates; they have become a burden to me. I am weary of bearing them" (1:13b–14). In Hosea, Yahweh is even more critical and promises to take action against these institutions: "I will put an end to all her mirth, her feasts, her new moons, her Sabbaths, and all her appointed feasts" (2:11).

Yes, the prophets are critical, but there is something important that the prophets *don't* do. They never say or describe Yahweh as saying, "I will put an end to *the* Sabbath." They always use Israel's possessive pronouns. In Isaiah, it's *your* new moons and *your* appointed feasts. In Hosea, it's *her* mirth, *her* feasts, *her* new moons, *her* Sabbaths, and all *her* appointed feasts. Compare that language with the language we see in Exodus: Above all, you shall keep *my* Sabbaths (31:13). And in Leviticus: They are *my* appointed feasts (23:2).

This is important because there are lots of Sabbaths.

Several historical-critical analyses of the Sabbath are illuminating here. In 1883, W. Lotz argued that the Hebrew word *shabbat* and the Akkadian word *shab/pattu(m)* both basically mean "day of rest," implying that the Akkadians had their own Sabbath practice. H. H. Robinson has tried to prove that Moses learned the Sabbath from the Kenites. A 1929 discovery told us that the Ugaritic calendar also has both seven-day and seven-year cycles.

The point of these studies is to remind us that, even though Yahweh was the first to rest on the seventh day, the *concept* of "the Sabbath" or the *practice* of periodic rest every seven days is neither unique to Israel nor original to the Bible. It is entirely imaginable that the Akkadians, Kenites, and Ugarits also had prophets like Isaiah and Hosea who criticized *their* sabbaths.

Israel's prophets don't criticize the Sabbath "in general" because there is no such thing. They don't criticize the Akkadians' Sabbath, the Kenites' Sabbath, or the Ugarits' Sabbath. They don't criticize Yahweh's Sabbath either. Yahweh criticizes

2 YOUR HOLIDAYS

Pharaoh's Sabbath and, through His prophets, He also criticizes *Israel's*.

Consider the way Frederick Douglass describes the way in which one of his masters, Mr. Edward Covey, kept "the holidays" in his household. Douglass doesn't criticize Christmas in general, but *Covey's* Christmas, which was a particular practice of the holiday in a particular household, indicative of holiday-keeping elsewhere in slave-holding Maryland. For reasons that will be made clear as this chapter continues, Frederick Douglass's voice is exceptionally helpful for reflecting on the relationship between history and holidays, the ways we keep them, and the ways we speak on them and about them. So he will be quoted here, and elsewhere, at some length:

> The days between Christmas and New Year's day are allowed as holidays; and, accordingly, we were not required to perform any labor, more than to feed and take care of the stock. This time we regarded as our own, by the grace of our masters; and we therefore used or abused it nearly as we pleased. Those of us who had families at a distance, were generally allowed to spend the whole six days in their society. This time, however, was spent in various ways. The staid, sober, thinking and industrious ones of our number would employ themselves in making corn-brooms, mats, horse-collars, and baskets; and another class of us would spend the time in hunting opossums, hares, and coons. But by far the larger part engaged in such sports and merriments as playing ball, wrestling, running foot-races, fiddling, dancing, and drinking whisky; and this latter mode of spending the time was by far the most agreeable to the feelings of our masters. A slave who would work during the holidays was considered by our masters as scarcely deserving them. He was regarded as one who rejected the favor of his master. It was deemed a disgrace not to get drunk at Christmas; and he was regarded as lazy indeed, who had not provided himself with the necessary means, during the year, to get whisky enough to last him through Christmas.

From what I know of the effect of these holidays upon the slave, I believe them to be among the most effective means in the hands of the slaveholder in keeping down the spirit of insurrection. Were the slaveholders at once to abandon this practice, I have not the slightest doubt it would lead to an immediate insurrection among the slaves. These holidays serve as conductors, or safety-valves, to carry off the rebellious spirit of enslaved humanity. But for these, the slave would be forced up to the wildest desperation; and woe betide the slaveholder, the day he ventures to remove or hinder the operation of those conductors! I warn him that, in such an event, a spirit will go forth in their midst, more to be dreaded than the most appalling earthquake.

The holidays are part and parcel of the gross fraud, wrong, and inhumanity of slavery. They are professedly a custom established by the benevolence of the slaveholders; but I undertake to say, it is the result of selfishness, and one of the grossest frauds committed upon the down-trodden slave. They do not give the slaves this time because they would not like to have their work during its continuance, but because they know it would be unsafe to deprive them of it. This will be seen by the fact, that the slaveholders like to have their slaves spend those days just in such a manner as to make them as glad of their ending as of their beginning. Their object seems to be, to disgust their slaves with freedom, by plunging them into the lowest depths of dissipation. For instance, the slaveholders not only like to see the slave drink of his own accord, but will adopt various plans to make him drunk. One plan is, to make bets on their slaves, as to who can drink the most whisky without getting drunk; and in this way they succeed in getting whole multitudes to drink to excess. Thus, when the slave asks for virtuous freedom, the cunning slaveholder, knowing his ignorance, cheats him with a dose of vicious dissipation, artfully labelled with the name of liberty. The most of us used to drink it down, and the result was just what might be supposed; many of us were led to think that there was little to choose between liberty and slavery. We felt, and very properly too, that we had almost as well be slaves to man as to rum. So, when the holidays ended, we staggered up from the filth of our wallowing, took a long breath, and marched to the field,—feeling, upon the whole, rather glad to go, from what our master had deceived us into a belief was freedom, back to the arms of slavery.[3]

Douglass's aim is not to dismantle the federal (and religious) holiday of Christmas but to expose the insidious form it took at the hands of the head of his household. Mr. Covey, like Pharaoh, and like any other person who inhabits a position of festal presidency over a community, is exactly whom the Sabbath Command addresses. Much like Douglass, what Israel's prophets are attacking is the sacrilege and injustice of these holidays as they are practiced.

Yahweh doesn't hate the Sabbath. He started it, and one of the main words He uses in His commandments is "keep." The word "keep," of course, has liturgical connotations, but we don't need to venture very far past its basic sense: Whatever else it means to "keep" something, at the very least, it means not getting rid of it.

On the Genre of "Festal Speech"

The second thesis is positive: *The Bible discloses the meaning of units of liturgical time in the famous words of Israel's presidents, both the words spoken on the holiday itself and other words spoken about what it means to remember and keep them.* I'm calling this genre of literature "festal speech." When we consider the meaning of the Passover, for example, we are quick to consider its institution narrative (Exod 12) and its fulfillment narrative (e.g., Luke 22), but we often forget to consider the great and famous speeches given by Israelite men on the Passover that developed for Israel, over the long course of her history, what that holiday had grown to mean. But before thinking about those speeches, consider a couple of festal speeches from the American holiday tradition, again from Douglass.

In 1871, Douglass gave his first festal speech on the holiday that was then called "Decoration Day," but that would later be renamed "Memorial Day" in 1882. The first thing to know about

---

3. Frederick Douglass, *Narrative of the Life of Frederick Douglass, An American Slave, Written by Himself* (Corkhill: The Anti-Slavery Office, 1845), 74–76.

Decoration Day is that it is connected to the Civil War (1861–1865). The second thing to know is that different people remember the Civil War differently.

On May 1, 1865, a group of manumitted slaves had gathered at a horse racetrack in Charleston, South Carolina, to honor the lives of 257 Union soldiers who had been imprisoned there. This was considered such a "good idea" in the popular American mind that more Americans began gathering on the first weekend of May each year in order to remember *more broadly* the bravery of American soldiers who had fallen in the great Civil War. Both Union and Confederate soldiers were commemorated for their bravery and sacrifice.

That is, until Douglass came down like Moses from Sinai and spoke words aimed, like the Levites' swords and like Peter's words at Pentecost, at the hearts of the people.

Douglass begins by stating what he considers the "problem" of this increasingly inclusive celebration: "We are sometimes asked in the name of patriotism ... to remember with equal admiration those who struck at the nation's life and those who struck to save it, those who fought for slavery and those who fought for liberty and justice."

He goes on to pose and answer the question: What would constitute a *right* remembrance of the Civil War?

> If we ought to forget a war which has filled our land with widows and orphans; which has made stumps of men of the very flower of our youth; which has sent them on the journey of life armless, legless, maimed, and mutilated; which has piled up a debt heavier than a mountain of gold, swept uncounted thousands of men into bloody graves and planted agony at a million hearthstones—I say, if this war is to be forgotten, I ask, in the name of all things sacred, *what shall men remember*? ....
>
> The essence and significance of our devotions here to-day are not to be found in the fact that the men whose remains fill these graves were brave in battle.... We are not here to applaud manly courage, save as it has been displayed in a noble cause. We must never forget that victory to the rebellion meant death

2 YOUR HOLIDAYS

to the republic. We must never forget that the loyal soldiers who rest beneath *this* sod flung themselves between the nation and the nation's destroyers.[4]

Douglass is an American prophet whose critical rhetoric echoes Hosea's: "*Your* Memorial Days I despise; I will put an end to them."

Douglass was asked to speak, seven years later, again on Decoration Day. This time it would be in Union Square, quite literally in the shadow of the recently-erected statue of Abraham Lincoln, whom Douglass begins his speech by naming "[America's] greatest soldier." This time around, he presses the same themes, insisting again upon the *moral meaning* of the holiday. And what distinguishes his rhetoric in *this* speech from his rhetoric in his previous one is his "liturgical development" of the holiday:

First, Douglass grounds the moral meaning of Memorial Day in the person and work of Abraham Lincoln. He calls people to act "in the spirit of the noble man whose image now looks down upon us," and then quotes from the final paragraph of his second inaugural address: Let us have "charity toward all, and malice toward none," and "Let us have peace." Douglass preaches that walking according to the spirit of Lincoln means not having malice toward slaveholders—"there is in my heart no malice toward the ex-slaveholders"—while also not forgetting that "there was a right side and a wrong side in the late war." He goes on, "While today we should have malice toward none, and charity toward all, it is no part of our duty to confound right with wrong."

Then, Douglass takes two other "sacred texts" from the American tradition: the Constitution and the Declaration. Taking the former, he exhorts his gathered congregation to keep the Law: "Let us have the Constitution, with its thirteenth, fourteenth, and fifteenth amendments, fairly interpreted, faithfully executed, and cheerfully obeyed in the fullness of their spirit and the completeness of their letter." Taking the latter, he characterizes the

---

4. Frederick Douglass, "Decoration Day," in *Frederick Douglass: Selected Speeches and Writings* (Chicago: Lawrence Hill, 2000).

SUNDAY

Declaration as the "broadest and grandest declaration of human rights the world has ever heard or read," contrasting it—as the psalmist compares the wisdom of the Torah to the laws of foreign nations—with the Confederacy, whose "pretended government" is "based upon an open, bold and shocking denial of all rights except the right of the strongest."[5]

What is Douglass doing in this Memorial Day speech? He is taking a newly-minted, underdeveloped federal holiday that commemorates a major event in his nation's moral history and tying it to key elements of the national canon: America's two chief founding documents; the epochal event of the Civil War; the pledge of commitment to the "eternal principles" of Equality, Liberty, and Justice demonstrated in the lives of the "loyal" Union soldiers; and the recent words from Abraham Lincoln, the "[great] soldier," who embodied those eternal principles in his own struggle as elected head of this historical body.

At the same time, he calls his fellow citizens to begin to participate in a particular "great work," which Lincoln had famously called an "unfinished work" at Gettysburg, by remembering their history rightly. The Church has her own "law of love" or "law of liberty." America has the never-ending work of establishing what Lincoln called "a just and a lasting peace."

Douglass sounds serious because calling Americans into the fullness of their celebratory traditions requires serious speech. Josef Pieper has a great little paragraph in his work on festivity that draws this out:

> Underlying all festive joy ... there has to be an absolutely universal affirmation extending to the world as a whole, to the reality of things and the existence of man himself. Naturally, this approval need not be a product of conscious reflection; it need not be formulated at all. Nevertheless, it remains the sole foundation for festivity, no matter what happens to be celebrated *in concreto*.... To reduce it to the most concise phrase, at bottom

---

5. Frederick Douglass, "Remembering the Civil War," in *Frederick Douglass: Selected Speeches and Writings*.

everything that is, is good, and it is good to exist.... Festivity, in its essential core, is nothing but the living out of this affirmation: *To celebrate a festival means to live out, for some special occasion and in an uncommon manner, the universal assent to the world as a whole.*[6]

Holidays *should* be characterized by the entire communion of participants nodding their heads in joyful affirmation, eating barbecue, and moving to happy music because "Life is Good." But Pieper also endorses the seriousness of Douglass's tone: "Such affirmation is not won by deliberately shutting one's eyes to the horrors in this world. Rather, it proves its seriousness by its confrontation with historical evil."[7]

On the Fourth of July, 1852, in Rochester, New York's Corinthian Hall, with President Millard Fillmore in attendance, Douglass told the gathered congregation that, "This, to you, is what the Passover was to the emancipated people of God. It carries your minds back to the day, and to the act of your great deliverance; and to the signs, and to the wonders, associated with that act, and that day."

He begins by calling the commemorated events to the people's remembrance: "With that blindness which seems to be the unvarying characteristic of tyrants, since Pharaoh and his hosts were drowned in the Red Sea, the British Government persisted in the exactions complained of." And then, in his rhetorical turn, which copies Hosea's use of possessive pronouns, he says in no uncertain terms that "This Fourth [of] July is *yours*, not *mine*. *You* may rejoice, *I* must mourn." He goes on to explain just why he cannot join in their Fourth of July celebrations:

> To drag a man in fetters into the grand illuminated temple of liberty, and call upon him to join you in joyous anthems, were inhuman mockery and sacrilegious irony. Do you mean, citizens, to mock me, by asking me to speak to-day? If so, there is a parallel to your conduct. And let me warn you that

---

6. Pieper, *In Tune with the World*, 2.
7. Pieper, *In Tune with the World*, 21.

it is dangerous to copy the example of a nation whose crimes, lowering up to heaven, were thrown down by the breath of the Almighty, burying that nation in irrecoverable ruin! ...

What, to the American slave, is your Fourth of July? I answer: a day that reveals to him, more than all other days in the year, the gross injustice and cruelty to which he is the constant victim. To him, your celebration is a sham; your boasted liberty, an unholy license; your national greatness, swelling vanity; your sounds or rejoicing are empty and heartless; your denunciation of tyrants, brass fronted impudence; your shouts of liberty and equality, hollow mockery; your prayers and hymns, your sermons and thanksgivings, with all your religious parade, and solemnity, are, to him, mere bombast, fraud, deception, impiety, and hypocrisy—a thin veil to cover up crimes which would disgrace a nation of savages....

It was fashionable, hundreds of years ago, for the children of Jacob to boast, we have "Abraham to our father," when they had long lost Abraham's faith and spirit. The people contented themselves under the shadow of Abraham's great name, while they repudiated the deeds which made his name great. Need I remind you that a similar thing is being done all over this country to-day? Need I tell you that the Jews are not the only people who built the tombs of the prophets, and garnished the sepulchres of the righteous? Washington could not die till he had broken the chains of his slaves. Yet his monument is built up by the price of human blood, and the traders in the bodies and souls of men shout— "We have Washington to our father." Alas that it should be so; yet so it is.[8]

Again, nowhere in his speech does Douglass tell America's legislative bodies to cross the Fourth of July off of their calendar or to set up a new holiday in its place. Douglass would have Americans continue to keep the feast, but to keep it rightly, as Paul tells the Corinthians (1 Cor 11:17–34).

What I hope to have shown through these excerpts from

---

8. Frederick Douglass, "What to the Slave Is the Fourth of July?," in *Frederick Douglass: Selected Speeches and Writings*.

Douglass's festal speeches is what the genre aims at accomplishing: The festal speech given by a presiding figure on a commemorative holiday is an occasion for fighting for the nation's memory and moral imagination.

One reason to quote Douglass's speeches at length here is to help us imagine that Israel's leaders also gave speeches during their major holidays and that, while many of those didn't make it into the Bible, some did, and we should read them. Moses, Hezekiah, and Josiah gave speeches on Passover. Jesus gave speeches on the Sabbath and the Passover. Peter gave a speech on Pentecost. Reading those texts as "festal speeches," which we will do in the following chapters, will help us understand how the Bible receives and develops Yahweh's holidays over the course of history.

On Ceremonially Taking Up the "Unfinished Work"

If it is the purview of some, like Frederick Douglass, to give "festal speeches," it is the purview of other presiding figures to make principled decisions that move their nation toward a fuller realization of the aspirational ideals embedded in the feasts themselves. That's why, for example, Israel moves from the Sabbath Command (Exod 20) to the Manumission Law (Exod 21) that realizes the principles of seventh-day rest in history.

The third thesis: *National holidays, both in the Bible and elsewhere, commemorate the progressive realization of that nation's ideals in their own history, and they stir people up to fill up the sufferings of their forebears, to finish their unfinished work, and to strive toward a future rest.*

I'll begin again with the Fourth of July.

There was no shortage of ceremony from the get-go. When John Adams wrote to Abigail that the Fourth "ought to be solemnized with pomp and parade, with shows, games, sports, guns, bells, bonfires, and illuminations … from this time forward forever more," he had fireworks in mind. Fireworks mattered.

On that date in 1777, thirteen fireworks were shot off in Philadelphia, and thirteen more in Boston. By 1783, private citizens bought their own fireworks to hold domestic commemorations of the anniversary. There were big, public fireworks shows and small, private fireworks shows.

Thomas Jefferson bent a Constitutional provision to its breaking point in order to buy the Louisiana Territory from a faltering France on April 30, 1803, effectively doubling the square acreage of the young nation. This deal had been three months in the making, and Jefferson was eager to announce his acquisition to the public. He had talked often in his letters and journals of his dream of watching his generation's descendants "spread themselves through the whole length of [the West] coast, covering it with free and independent Americans, unconnected with us, and enjoying like us the rights of self-government."[9]

Jefferson had a distinct vision for an America whose independence was grounded in an economy of virtuous agrarian producers. Purchasing Louisiana was an enormous step toward realizing his moral vision. But he waited until the Fourth of July to make the announcement in order to frame the purchase as a patriotic act, extending the yet-unrealized American ideals of 1776 over more space.

Just four years prior, New York State had celebrated the Fourth with a word of pardon. On July 4, 1799, the state declared *partial* emancipation to her slaves, granting gradual freedom by offering contracts of indentured servitude to all enslaved children who were born on or after the Fourth of that year.

Why the Fourth? Again, for ceremonial reasons.

Twenty-eight years later, on July 4, 1827, New York fulfilled this gesture by proclaiming *full* emancipation to those same people. This proclamation was so effective that the 1830 census shows not a single slave remaining held in the state.

July 4, 1827 was an enormous victory for enslaved African-Americans in New York, but it proved not to be enough to redeem fifty years of stale ceremony. Remember what Douglass had said twenty-five years later in 1852: The Fourth is "yours, not mine."

---

9. Thomas Jefferson, "Thomas Jefferson to John Jacob Astor, 24 May 1812," in *The Papers of Thomas Jefferson*, Retirement Series, vol. 5, ed. J. Jefferson Looney (Princeton: Princeton University Press, 2008), 74–75.

2 YOUR HOLIDAYS

The men, women, and children emancipated by New York's proclamation instead organized a celebratory parade for July 5. It was ceremonially significant that the Fifth of July parade directly followed the Fourth of July fireworks. By Douglass's time, few enough states had followed New York's lead that Douglass still could not see the Fourth of July as a holiday that African-Americans could celebrate.

Over time, the Fourth of July accumulated meaning, and that's my point. America's presidents have acquired more territory, incorporated more states, fought in more wars, and addressed the nation in the wake of many more tragedies and trials. America's founding principles of "Liberty, Equality, and Justice" or "the pursuit of happiness" are no longer abstract and aspirational ideals for the future, but ideals that have taken on fuller and more distinctly American shapes over time. Enfleshed ideals.

The point isn't that American liberty is perfect liberty, but that, here, in America, the common value of liberty has taken a distinctly and meaningfully American shape. When Americans talk about political and economic liberty, we talk about it in the context of the American Revolution, our federal system, the century of Westward Expansion, the story of racial slavery and progressive emancipation, equal voting rights for adults, and economic liberty in the age of superwealth.

The African country of Liberia, for one, which began as an American colony, also values Liberty, but it has taken on a different form in their history. The Asian country of Bhutan values the "the pursuit of happiness" so much that their economists replaced GDP with a new metric called "Gross National Happiness," or GNH, as the primary economic metric of success.

The Fourth of July doesn't celebrate perfect liberty, or liberty fully realized. It commemorates the events within which one particular people in history has struggled to realize its moral ideals at home and abroad, in its own way, against tyrants of every shape and size.

Holidays, and the national values they commemorate, accumulate meaning over history.

SUNDAY

By the time the evangelists tell the story of Jesus picking heads of grain and telling the religious leaders that it is better to save life on the Sabbath than to destroy it (Luke 6:9), it is the next link in a chain of commemorative events that includes David eating the consecrated bread (1 Sam 21) and Mattathias stirring up Israel to defend themselves against the Seleucids: "Let us wage war against any man who comes upon us for war on the Sabbath day" (1 Macc 2:41).

According to "time scholars," this way of thinking about holidays—as recurring opportunities for progressive fulfillment of ideals—is characteristic of the Old Testament. While it is well known that ancient cultures emphasized the "cyclical" nature of time and that modern cultures emphasize the "linear" or "progressive" nature of time, the Scriptures depict time as both cyclical *and* linear. Israel keeps a recurring liturgical calendar, attending to time's cyclicity; but she is also characteristically oriented toward the realization of a just and peaceable future.

Douglas Estes, a scholar of time, describes Old Testament history as "linear time with eternal recurrence," by which he means that "the same events repeat themselves in the same pattern at different times."[10] That's why the Sabbath is not just a commemoration but also a peaceful, legislated reenactment of the Exodus. The Sabbath accumulates meaning over time. And it's also why Israel has such a participatory notion of the Passover: "In every generation a person must see himself as if he has [just] come out of Egypt" (Mishnah Pesachim 10.5).

In one of his three books on Israel's concepts of time and timing, time scholar Sacha Stern makes a similar observation: "The annual observance of the Passover would have been supported by the belief that the events commemorated on this date were being somehow re-enacted or were occurring again." Even more on the nose, he argues that "particular days of the calendar, especially

---

10. Douglas Estes, *The Temporal Mechanics of the Fourth Gospel: A Theory of Hermeneutical Relativity in the Gospel of John*, Biblical Interpretation (Leiden: Brill, 2008), 41.

festival and fast days, are designated for the historical or eschatological recurrence of analogous events."[11]

This makes sense. Yahweh rested on the seventh day, and He continues to do so every seventh day. We participate in that rest every seventh day, by resting and granting rest, expecting Yahweh to continue granting rest to all of us until the day when all things are set right.

Yahweh delivered Israel from Egypt during Passover. And then He continues to deliver them from other enemies at the same time as Passover.

At one level, every time Yahweh delivers, it's like a new Exodus and a new Passover, and the next celebration of Passover will *include* a celebration of that latest deliverance.

At another level, the Scriptures show Yahweh's peculiar tendency to deliver His people *during* the days leading up to Passover.

After years of these patterns of deliverance—similar in character and in timing—the Passover accumulates patterned meaning. Passover meant a lot in Exodus 12, and it meant even more the following year when Moses celebrated it. They had their deliverance from Egypt to be thankful for, and then they also had a whole year with Yahweh at Sinai to give even more thanks for. It stands to reason that most Israelites celebrated the Passover most years. And then when Joshua celebrated it by the Jordan, it meant Egypt plus Sinai plus every year of desert wandering. By the time Jesus celebrated the Passover, the meaning of Passover was ripe, or full: "When the fullness of time had come, God sent forth his Son" (Gal 4:4).

The fact that the New Testament pays such specific attention to how Jesus keeps Israel's festal calendar should make our spidey-senses tingle for at least a few reasons. First, Jesus, like Frederick Douglass, is a festal speaker. He is sometimes called upon and at other times takes it upon Himself to speak commemorative,

---

11. Sacha Stern, *Time and Process in Ancient Judaism* (Oxford: Littman Library of Jewish Civilization, 2003), 46.

SUNDAY

critical, and inspiring words on holidays. Second, Jesus, like Thomas Jefferson, is a president—not in the technical sense, as the elected executive of a republic, but in the more common sense, as one who presides over things.

When Jesus fulfills the Law, He doesn't just fulfill the moral law, by honoring His father and mother (Exod 20:12; cf. John 19:25–27); and He doesn't just fulfill the ceremonial law, by being circumcised on the eighth day (Lev 12:3; cf. Luke 1:59); but He also fulfills laws that are reserved for extraordinary occasions. Leviticus 23:4, for example, commands Moses to proclaim Yahweh's feasts at their appointed times. Everyone can honor their father and mother, and all boys can be circumcised, but only "presidents" proclaim feasts. And perhaps only Jesus can do what He did in the synagogue and Nazareth, when He opened the book of Isaiah and proclaimed the Year of the Lord's Favor (Luke 4:16–19).

What Jesus does during the holidays, the way He keeps time, is part of His ministry of doing only what He sees His Father doing (John 5:19). It's worth noting that the concept of doing what one sees his father doing is not novel. That's just one of the places where the principles of conservatism and progressivism overlap. It's why Lincoln started his address at Gettysburg by situating their present work in the context of the fathers' labor: "Fourscore and seven years ago our fathers brought forth on this continent, a new nation, conceived in Liberty, and dedicated to the proposition that all men are created equal. Now we are engaged in a great civil war, testing whether that nation, or any nation so conceived and so dedicated, can long endure."[12] And it's why, as he accepted a second nomination for the presidency from his party, Franklin Delano Roosevelt framed his project as a reaffirmation and restoration of the fathers' vision: "[Philadelphia] is fitting ground on which to reaffirm the faith of our fathers; to pledge ourselves to restore to the people a wider freedom; to give to 1936 as the founders gave to 1776—an American way of life."[13] Per John, the

---

12. Abraham Lincoln, "The Gettysburg Address," in *America's Most Famous Speeches*, ed. Frank Ballard (New York: Random House, 1984).

13. Franklin D. Roosevelt, "Acceptance Speech for the Re-Nomination for the

Pharisees said, "Abraham is our father," which Jesus understood well enough to respond, "If you were Abraham's children, you would be doing the works Abraham did" (8:39–40). For all His challenges to the religious establishment—the Pharisees' presidency over and stewardship of Israel's historic institutions—Jesus identifies Himself as the true conservative. He inaugurated His kingship by restoring Israel's institutions to the purposes for which Yahweh intended them.

The Pharisees weren't shocked that Jesus framed His presidency as doing what He saw His Father doing. They were shocked that He claimed to know and see God, to be from Him, and to equate acceptance of Him with acceptance of the Father, and all of their forefathers, and rejection of Him with rejection of the same. Jesus spoke as one with authority, the kind of authority that belongs to the God who rested on the seventh day of creation and delivered Israel from Egypt in the first place.

On One Way That Scripture Emphasizes Liturgical Time

The fourth thesis is a hermeneutical observation: *Oftentimes, the Bible brings attention to units of liturgical time by framing stories with "liturgical time markers."*

The Bible is more interested in "timing" than in "time."

Time is abstract. Timing is concerned with how we understand certain activities, events, or eras in relationship to other ones. And "time markers" are adverbial phrases at the beginning of narratives, either short narratives or long ones, that relate the activity, event, or era in that particular narrative with another one outside of it.

One famous time marker is the one that starts Isaiah 6: "In the year that King Uzziah died." Consider the author's other options. For one, he could have used a number. He might not have said, "In the year 740 BC," because that way of counting didn't exist yet, but plenty of contemporary cultures counted years in numbers.

Presidency," Philadelphia, Pennsylvania, June 27, 1936, available at http://www.presidency.ucsb.edu/ws/?pid=15314.

SUNDAY

For another, he could have chosen another major event that happened that year. Lots of things happened the year King Uzziah died, which we know because, well, lots of things happen every year.

The author chooses to begin this particular narrative with the time marker, "In the year King Uzziah" died because there is a meaningful relationship between the referential event—the death of King Uzziah—and the narrated event—Isaiah's encounter with Yahweh. Temporal markers like this one present Bible readers with fun hermeneutical puzzles: Why does the text pair these two events?

In many cases, such as this one, the relationship between the events is deeply meaningful. Uzziah died with leprosy he contracted when, out of pride, he entered Yahweh's temple and tried to burn incense. Isaiah, by contrast, sees Yahweh surrounded by His "burning ones" (6:2), the house fills with smoke (v. 4), a burning coal takes his guilt away (v. 7), and he is commissioned to preach to a guilty Israel until it has burned (v. 12). The book of Isaiah presents the prophet Isaiah as some kind of a priestly replacement of Uzziah the king.

Temporal markers don't just tell readers *when* an event happens. They imply that a relationship exists between a specific external event and the event at hand.

And the Bible is full of temporal markers. Genesis 1:1–2:3 tells the story of the first Sabbath and why we keep it. Exodus 12 tells Israel how, when, and why to celebrate the Passover. Israel tells Ruth's story during the barley harvest and puts on productions of Esther at Purim.

In his study of temporal markers in the Old Testament, Michael LeFebvre concludes that "Dates are added to certain events for their liturgical remembrance, not as journalistic details."[14] The texts include dates "to aid the needful worshiper; and not ... the curious historian."[15]

---

14. Michael LeFebvre, *The Liturgy of Creation: Understanding Calendars in Old Testament Context* (Downers Grove: Intervarsity Press, 2019), 60.

15. LeFebvre, *The Liturgy of Creation*, 107.

2 YOUR HOLIDAYS

What I think has gone underappreciated in our Bible reading is the fact that the historical narratives of the New Testament—the Gospels and Acts—are also using temporal markers to relate the events they narrate to other times outside the text. Sometimes, the external referents are fixed times, like this extended one early on in Luke: "In the fifteenth year of the reign of Tiberius Caesar, Pontius Pilate being governor of Judea, and Herod being tetrarch of Galilee, and his brother Philip tetrarch of the region of Iturea and Trachonitis, and Lysanias tetrarch of Abilene, during the high priesthood of Annas and Caiaphas…" (3:1–2).

At other times, the external referents are the festal institutions or *recurring* events I referenced above. The external referent in one of Luke's first time markers is actually a recurring liturgical one. "In the days of Herod the King," referring to a historical era, "there was a priest named Zechariah, of the division of Abijah" (1:5). In the important story about Zechariah, Luke takes care to mention that the event happens "while he was serving as priest before God when his division was on duty, according to the custom of the priesthood" (1:8).

Why? Luke wasn't just being a thorough historian; he was participating in the Scriptural tradition of relating the events he narrated to meaningful events elsewhere in the Bible.

Zechariah was a member of the priestly division of Abijah who, among the twenty-four priestly divisions listed in 1 Chronicles 24:7–18, was assigned to serve eighth. The details of their service are spelled out in 23:28–32. Israel divided their twelve-moon year into forty-eight weeks, which meant each of the twenty-four divisions served the same two weeks each year. Abijah's division served the fourth weeks of the months Ziv and Bul.

This is significant because it had been during the fourth week of Ziv—that is, during Abijah's service—that Israel had delivered herself from Antiochus IV Epiphanes of the Seleucids (1 Macc 13:51). Israel's deliverance from the Seleucids is especially interesting because of its relationship with the Sabbath. The Seleucids' conquest of Israel was made possible only because, when they attacked, the Jews refused to take up arms on the Sabbath

(2:35–38). Under the leadership of Mattathias, a priest famous for his principled observance of the law, Israel decided to permit self-defense on the Sabbath: "Let us wage war against any man who comes upon us for war on the Sabbath day" (2:41).

Luke relates the very first story he tells to a time when Israel commemorated Mattathias's decision to "save life" on the Sabbath rather than "to destroy it" (Luke 6:9).

Finding meaning in adverbial phrases like this one encourages readers to consider more curiously the moments in which New Testament texts refer explicitly to the recurring liturgical times that constitute Israel's calendar. Jesus speaks and acts on the Sabbath, during the Passover, and "on the first day of the week." In every instance that these New Testament texts introduce Jesus' words and works by framing them with a recurring liturgical time, they present Jesus as meaningfully receiving and developing that unit of liturgical time, in line with all of the people before Him whom the Old Testament texts depict as speaking and acting within those special times.

The Church doesn't receive Israel's calendar as her own. We don't keep the Passover as the Passover, or the Feast of Tabernacles as the Feast of Tabernacles. We don't mark off every Seventh Year as a Sabbath Year the way Israel aspired to.

But the Church keeps Sunday as her recurring weekly feast, and what Sunday means to us is a lot like what the Sabbath means to Israel, although it is not identical.

Like the Sabbath, Sunday is a day of rest, but not just a "day," and not just of "rest." It is a commemorative feast—of the historical event of Jesus' resurrection—with the ceremonial and moral power to give shape to the Church's annual calendar and her ethics every bit as much as the Sabbath gave shape to Israel's calendar and ethics. Chapter 3 will pay attention to the ways in which Luke uses the Sabbath as a time marker.

Sundays also commemorate Jesus' death, and in our celebrations of the Eucharist (or Holy Communion or the Lord's Supper), we also make Sunday into a weekly reenactment of the Passover over which Jesus presided. Chapter 4 will pay attention to the

2 YOUR HOLIDAYS

ways in which Luke participates in the tradition of telling Passover stories.

Sunday is also the day that all four New Testament historians call "the first day of the week" (Matt 28:1; Mark 16:2; Luke 24:1; John 20:1). Bible readers often forget that "the first day of the week" does not simply refer to one day's position within a seven-day period, but is a shorthand reference to a particular feast day that already existed in Israel's annual calendar (Lev 23). Chapter 5 will discuss the subtle ways in which the New Testament draws upon one of Israel's rather minor feasts to frame liturgically the death and resurrection of Jesus Christ.

3 SABBATH HERO

"The Spirit of the Lord is upon me ... to proclaim the year of the Lord's favor."
Luke 4:18–19

"The Son of Man is Lord of the Sabbath."
Luke 6:5

The Scriptures authorized God's ministers to set aside the seventh day of each week as "holy" and "a Sabbath" and to call all of God's people together for gathered, ceremonial worship.[1] This worship commemorates all of God's works of creation—especially The Creation (Exod 20:11)—and of new creation—especially The Exodus (Deut 5:15). This worship includes the ritual reading of Scriptures, the saying of prayers, and the offering of offerings. It characterizes the people of God as distinct from other peoples, and it reminds God's people that He is distinct from other gods.

Sunday is a Sabbath,[2] but it is on the first day of the week

---

1. Some people object to the claim that Israel was called to worship in an organized, recognizable way on the seventh day. In lieu of an argument, I would point them to the description of the Sabbath offering in Numbers 28:9–10, which I am sure those who object to this claim will already have read and explained away.

2. Some people object to this, too, appealing to Romans 14 and classifying "food

3 SABBATH HERO

rather than the seventh, and while it celebrates God's work of newly creating Israel out of Egypt, it commemorates a different historical act of new creation: Jesus' resurrection. The Church believes that what God did by raising Jesus from the dead, He has already extended to us by raising us with Him and making us new creations, and that one day the whole cosmos will die and be raised as a new creation—a "new heavens and a new earth." In the meantime, we commemorate all of God's other acts of raising dead things, and we give Him thanks for them.

And the New Testament gives us even *more* to remember. In Genesis 2, God rests on the seventh day, and we rest only by following the pattern of and participating in that rest. In the New Testament, authors like Luke give us more stories of God, in Christ, keeping the same Sabbath that He instituted and legislated. This chapter considers how Jesus keeps the Sabbath in order to help us think about how we can follow His pattern and participate in that rest. And, ultimately, to think about what Sunday means.

The way Luke tells the story, Jesus kicks off His ministry on the Sabbath. Neither of the high priests, Annas or Caiaphas, was able to be there. Nor were the Judaean prefect, Marcus Pontius Pilate, or the Galilean tetrarch, Herod Antipater. Jesus didn't even do it in the temple.

But Luke says that it was "on the Sabbath" in Nazareth of Galilee, "where he had been brought up," and, according to "his custom," that Jesus went to the local synagogue and offered a succinct Sabbatical oration. When the scroll of Isaiah was handed to Him, He ran His finger along the text until He found "the place where it was written," and then He read the following lines from Isaiah. Naturally, there are seven of them:

---

laws" and "the Sabbath" in the same category. But if they are so unwilling to grant me this premise—that the Scriptures exhort Christians themselves to weekly worship—I don't imagine they'll find much use in this book, which seeks to draw out its significance. Still, I would remind them of my claim from the previous chapter—that the Sabbath is neither a moral, nor a ceremonial, nor a judicial law, but a religious metaphysics of time—and invite them to consider my discussion of other seemingly "anti-Sabbath" New Testament texts in the remainder of this chapter.

SUNDAY

> "The Spirit of the Lord is upon me,
>   because he has anointed me
>   to proclaim good news to the poor.
> He has sent me to proclaim liberty to the captives
>   and recovering of sight to the blind,
>   to set at liberty those who are oppressed,
> to proclaim the year of the Lord's favor." (4:18–19)

Much of the meaning of this text is right on the surface. Post-baptism and fresh out of the wilderness, Jesus is anointed by the Spirit to proclaim four things: good news to the poor; liberty to the captives; recovery of sight to the blind; and the year of the Lord's favor, evidently to everyone. The only non-*proclamatory* action in this list is His "[setting] at liberty" of "those who are oppressed." He both *proclaims* liberty and *sets at* liberty. He says "proclaim" two times and "liberty" two times. And the word *aphesis*, here translated "liberty," is more commonly translated "release," which I have already argued is the main meaning of the Sabbath in the Old Testament.

This means that what Jesus proclaims is consistent with the Scriptures' Big Vision of the Sabbath. For Jesus, the Sabbath doesn't mean only "rest" in general, but rest by means of release and restoration, along the lines of Seventh Year and Sabbath Year manumission laws (Exod 21 and Deut 15, respectively) and the Year of Jubilee laws about the restoration of persons and property (Lev 25). Reading Jesus' lines—"liberty to the captives" and "year of the Lord's favor"—with these Old Testament passages in mind, it looks very much like keeping the Sabbath means something more to Jesus than simply "not doing work" on the last day of each week.

By the time He had finished His text, sat down, and said some words about Elisha, "all in the synagogue were filled with wrath," and they tried to drive Him off a cliff (4:28–30). But Jesus is *not* driven off a cliff. He comes back on another Sabbath and does all of the Sabbath things that He said He would do. And He expands on the themes of His proclamation in His teaching. This chapter will unpack Jesus' Sabbath proclamation, His Sabbath teachings, and His Sabbath actions.

Proclaiming the Big Sabbath

Jesus' Big Sabbath Proclamation raises a very real question that no one talks about: What must it have been like to be the guy whose job it would have been to do the reading the next week? The reason no one talks about this problem is probably that it was only a problem for that one guy, and Luke didn't bother to put his story in his Gospel.

Whoever he was, and whatever he was about, we can infer from Luke that, since he was probably there that day, this man too was "filled with wrath." At some point that day, after trying to drive Jesus off a cliff, he must have walked home for at least a couple of minutes. What went through his mind as he did? How was he going to follow up that, well, whatever that was from Joseph's son? Should he address it out loud? Or should he just pause, look up, and swivel a knowing glance around the congregation to emphasize how much *less* provocative his reading was going to be?

How did Jesus' claims sit with this man over the course of the next week? Jesus explicitly said that it was "the year of the Lord's favor" now. Who did Jesus think He was, taking it upon Himself to announce the arrival of a new era (Lev 23:4)? Sure, several lectionaries had this text from Isaiah read at the turning of the year, and it's a well-known and well-loved theme, but what did Jesus mean that it was "fulfilled" in their hearing?

But the most interesting question he must have faced, and the one that the text forces on its readers, is why Jesus got some of the words wrong. Why did He stop halfway through the sentence and not finish the second verse: "The year of the Lord's favor *and* the day of vengeance of our God"? That's a puzzle. And then why did He skip over the line "bind up the broken-hearted"? It was right there in the scroll. Did Jesus get nervous and skip a line, or does He have some vendetta against compassionate responses to grief? And what was He getting at by adding that line, "to release those who are oppressed" from Isaiah 58?

SUNDAY

Jesus doesn't exactly *misquote* Isaiah, but it's true that the Greek text of Luke 4:18–19 doesn't exactly match the LXX (the "Septuagint," which is the name for the commonly accepted Greek translation of the Old Testament) translation of Isaiah 61:1–2a.

From one angle, Jesus is a bad Bible reader. Your main job is just to not get the words wrong. But to readers of faith, Jesus is up to something, and the meaning is in the details.

Here are the facts: *Luke's Gospel presents the Church with a Jesus who announces His ministry program by offering a heavily revised version of a popular passage from Isaiah.* The premise of this chapter is that there is *meaning* in these differences, and the first step of this chapter will be to poke around and try to understand why Luke records these differences for his readers. Sometimes it helps to see familiar words in a different language to notice what's different, so here they are in Greek, with the differences underlined:

Isaiah 61:1a (LXX)
Pneuma kuriou ep' eme
hou heineken echrisen me
euangelisasthai ptōchois.
Apestalken me iasasthai tous suntetrimmenous tē kardia
kēruchai aichmalōtois aphesin
kai tuphlois anablepsin
kalesai eniauton kuriou dekton.

Luke 4:18–19
Pneuma kuriou ep' eme
hou heineken echrisen me
euangelisasthai ptōchois.
Apestalken me kēruchai aichmalōtois aphesin
kai tuphlois anablepsin
aposteilai tethrausmenous en aphesei (from Isa 58:6)
kēruchai eniauton kuriou dekton.

The first three lines of the two texts are identical. Then in the fourth line, which is the center-most and longest line, Jesus removes the words "to bind up the broken-hearted" and bumps the words "to proclaim release to the captives" up from line 5, moving them to the center. The next line matches the source. Then He inserts the phrase, "to release those who are oppressed," which comes from Isaiah 58:6. In the seventh and final line, Jesus switches out one word that means "proclaim" (*kalesai*) for another one that also means "proclaim" (*kēruchai*). I'll take these revisions in order:

Why add a line from Isaiah 58?

Isaiah 58 is a famous chapter in which Yahweh reminds Israel of the *ethical* quality of liturgical time. Two chapters earlier, He had made a liturgical invitation and promise: "Everyone who keeps the Sabbath and does not profane it, and holds fast my covenant—these I will bring to my holy mountain, and make them joyful in my house of prayer" (56:6–7). This echoes Exodus 31:13: "Above all, keep my Sabbaths."

In order to clarify the terms for any rich young rulers or contractually-minded lawyers in the audience, He goes on in chapter 58 to spell out what He means by the words "and does not profane it" by explaining how Israel is currently profaning the Sabbath: "Behold, in the day of your fast you seek your own pleasure, and oppress all your workers" (58:3). In the verses that follow, He unpacks the positive sense of "keeping the Sabbath" and "true fasts," listing eight admonitions from which Jesus, or any other festal speaker who wished to reground the popular understanding of a holiday in its moral meaning, could choose. Here they are:

> To loose the bonds of wickedness,
> to undo the straps of the yoke,
> *to let the oppressed go free,*
> and to break every yoke....
> to share your bread with the hungry
> and bring the homeless poor into your house;
> when you see the naked, to cover him,
> and not to hide yourself from your own flesh. (vv. 6–7)

Do *these* things, says Yahweh and—famously echoed by Felix Mendelssohn's chorus in the rousing "Elijah," Op. 70. No. 42—"Then shall your light break forth like the dawn, and your healing shall spring up speedily" (v. 9). Isaiah 58 closes with some conclusory comments on keeping the Sabbath rightly: "If you turn back your foot from the Sabbath, from doing *your* pleasure on *my* holy day, and call the Sabbath a delight and the holy day of Yahweh honorable ... then you shall take delight in Yahweh, and I will make you ride on the heights of the earth" (vv. 13–14).

This chapter builds the reader's anticipation for the revelation of the "anointed one" who is also the speaker at Isaiah 61—the one with the ministry of four happy proclamations: good news to the poor, liberty to the captives, recovery of sight to the blind, and the year of the Lord's favor to all.

Jesus was a brilliant Bible reader, but not all of His exegetical moves were His original ideas. In the case of this controversial Sabbath Day reading, He probably wasn't the first person to combine Isaiah 58 and 61 in a single reading. So who *was* the first to combine them, and why?

Well, we don't know who was first, but we do know something about Israel's tradition of combining the texts. Rabbi Marc Tannenbaum has written about Israel's association of Isaiah 58, a passage about the Sabbath Year, with Jubilee themes.[3] For what it's worth, there is a near consensus among Old Testament scholars that Isaiah 58 has the Sabbath Year in view and that Isaiah 61 has an eschatologized Year of Jubilee in view. One commentator, in a discussion of the eight admonitions in 58:6–7, finds them to be an "exceptionally penetrating and emphatic admonition ... to the individual Israelite," which explains how the "Big Picture" proclamation of release in 61:1–2 was to be worked out practically in the world.[4]

---

3. Marc H. Tannenbaum, "Holy Year 1975 and Its Origins in the Jewish Jubilee Year," *Jubilaeum 7* (1974), 65.

4. Claus Westermann, *Isaiah 40–66*, trans. D.M.G. Stalker (Philadephia: Westminster, 1969), 337, cited in Patrick D. Miller, "An Exposition of Luke 4:16–21," *Interpretation 67* (2013): 419.

In short, doing Isaiah 58 is *how* Isaiah 61 happens. Isaiah 58 lists the "highways to Zion." When Israel *performs* the admonitions of Isaiah 58, the result is the realization of Isaiah 61. Isaiah 58 is ethics; Isaiah 61 is eschatology.

The tradition of associating these two chapters—and the three levels of the Sabbath—is preserved in a text from the Qumran community, which scholars call 11QMelchizedek (11QMelch). This text, discovered by Adam S. Van der Woude in 1965, uses Isaiah 61:1–3 as a base pattern into which a series of other biblical texts are woven. 11QMelch cites a number of texts—Leviticus 25:13 (Year of Jubilee), Deuteronomy 15:2 (Sabbath Year), Isaiah 52:7 (Servant Song), and Psalms 82 and 7—linking them together based on their lexical relationships to Isaiah 61:1–3.

11QMelch proclaims the "year of grace of Melchizedek and of his armies" (1.9), who are identified with the *elohim* (1.8; cf. Psa 82:6). In this year, Melchizedek will "carry out the vengeance of God's judgments" (1.13; cf. Isa 61:2b) and release all the captives (1.4, 13, 25) "from the hand of Belial," their captor (1.13, 25), as well as from the moral and sacrificial debt of all their iniquities (1.6).

So by the time Jesus stood up in a synagogue in Nazareth on the Sabbath Day, there was already a tradition that anticipated a divine figure, flanked by heavenly armies, who would proclaim an eschatological Year of Jubilee characterized by the Sabbath Year's ethics of "release" from captivity and sins (11QMelch 1.3; cf. *aphesis*, LXX Deut 15:2; Isa 58:6). The ethics provide the shape of the eschatology.

This tradition has led me to make three conclusions about Jesus and the Sabbath, which I offer here. First, Jesus fulfills both the canonical Scriptures *and* Israel's hope for a Melchizedekian figure who would lead his armies into a war-like campaign of manumission and forgiveness. This tradition invites readers to understand Jesus as a Sabbath President: leading armies, calling times, and declaring pardons. Second, Jesus does not take the Sabbath to be an isolated command that deals only with the abstract notion of "rest" on "the seventh day." He treats the Sabbath in the fuller sense that we read above, taking the Sabbath as a Big Deal—that is, as fundamentally connected to the economic concerns of the Sabbath Year and the Year of Jubilee. Third, as Douglass did on the Fourth of July, Jesus uses these two texts in Isaiah to reground the gathered people's understanding of what their holiday calendar *means*, both historically and morally.

But why add **that** line from Isaiah 58?

The fact is that He had eight good lines to choose from, and it seems as if any one of them would have done the trick. But the question of why *that* line is actually a pretty simple one to answer, with essentially no scholarly controversy: Jesus chooses the one line with the word *aphesis* in it. I can't explain this any better than Patrick Miller did in the conclusion of his article on this passage:

> The tie that binds Isaiah 61:1–2 and 58:6 together in Luke 4 is the small word *aphesis*, the word translated "release" for the captives and "liberty" for the oppressed.... It is the catchword binding the two quotations together. Out of the four sentences in Isaiah 58:6 that all say essentially the same thing, the one chosen here in the gospel quotation is the one that in the Greek translation uses *aphesis*.[5]

So *aphesis* serves a practical purpose: It connects the two chapters. But does it do more than that?

It would seem so. This word *aphesis* appears seventeen times in the New Testament, and ten (!) of these occurrences appear in Luke and Acts. The point is, Luke likes the word. In Mary's song, it is *aphesis* from sins which gives God's people the "knowledge of salvation" (Luke 1:77); John preaches a baptism of repentance for the *aphesis* of sins (3:3); Jesus proclaims *aphesis* to the captives and *aphesis* for the oppressed (4:18), and He tells His disciples that "it is written that the Christ would suffer and rise from the dead on the third day, and that *aphesis* for the forgiveness of sins would be proclaimed in his name to all nations" (24:46–47).

---

5. Miller, "Exposition of Luke 4:16–21," 420.

3 SABBATH HERO

Five times in Acts, various preachers repeat that phrase, "*aphesis* of sins" (2:38; 5:31; 10:43; 13:38; 26:18).

On the Sabbath in Galilee, Jesus proclaims a ministry program of Sabbath *aphesis*. He will proclaim "release" to the captives and the oppressed. He will "release," and He will authorize His heavenly army of disciples to "release," people from demons, debts, and even death itself. What's more, when He talks about His plans with Moses and Elijah on the Mount of Transfiguration, He describes what He is doing as an "exodus"; the three men "spoke of his *exodon* which He was about to accomplish at Jerusalem" (9:31).

Why bump "bind up the brokenhearted" and include "the recovering of sight to the blind"?

Isaiah 61:1 says that the anointed one will "bind up the brokenhearted," and that *would* have been the fourth of seven lines in Jesus' proclamation in Luke 4:18–19. The immediate effect of bumping that phrase is to bring two parts of a single grammatical clause from Isaiah closer together. Here's how it reads in Isaiah:

> He has sent me to bind up the brokenhearted, to proclaim liberty to the captives, and the opening of the prison to those who are bound.

Now, I don't have a grammatical argument so much as I have a rhetorical one. The grammatical essence of the sentence is that some subject, "Yahweh," expressed with the word "He," has done something, which is "sent me." The mission of the sent one, which is also the purpose of Yahweh's sending of him, is expressed in two infinitive phrases, the first of which begins with "to bind up" and the second of which begins with "to proclaim." And the sent one is sent to proclaim two things: liberty to captives and prison-opening to bound-ones. This feels especially nice in the English Standard Version since the brokenhearted are being "bound up," but liberty is being proclaimed to the "bound." (Great work, ESV!)

My observation is that the sentence takes on new force and

new focus when the first infinitive phrase is passed over. In Luke, Isaiah's sentence now begins this way:

> He has sent me ~~to bind up the brokenhearted~~, to proclaim *aphesis* to the captives ...

The point is not at all that Jesus is unconcerned with people who have broken hearts. It's just that Jesus *immediately* follows the words, "He has sent me," with the keywords, "to proclaim *aphesis*." And then He adds a line from Isaiah 58:6 that reads, both in the LXX of Isaiah 61:1 and in Luke 4:18, "to proclaim to the prisoners *aphesis*." Jesus absolutely binds up the brokenhearted, but in Luke 4, the reason Yahweh sent Him is Sabbath-themed "unbinding."

*Why bump the LXX's word for "proclaim" (**kalesai**) for another word for "proclaim" (**kēruchai**) at 4:19?*

Okay, this is an extra credit point. The short version is that Jesus uses a different word for "proclaim" than the LXX of Isaiah does, and it's one that strengthens the connection between Isaiah 61 and Leviticus 25. This gives the reader the impression that when Jesus proclaims "the Acceptable Year," He is *definitely* proclaiming the Year of Jubilee. And it reinforces just how central *aphesis*/"release" is to His proclamation.

Jesus uses the word *kēruchai*, translated "to proclaim," two times in Luke 4:18–19. Here's the passage again:

> The Spirit of the Lord is upon me,
> because he has anointed me
> to proclaim good news to the poor.
> He has sent me to proclaim (*kēruchai*) liberty to the captives
> and recovering of sight to the blind,
> to set at liberty those who are oppressed,
> to proclaim (*kēruchai*) the year of the Lord's favor.

This repetition wouldn't be terribly noteworthy, except that it is another unexpected departure from the LXX of Isaiah 61:1–2a, copied again here:

> The Spirit of the Lord God is upon me,
> because the Lord has anointed me
> to bring good news to the poor;
> he has sent me to bind up the brokenhearted,
> to proclaim (*kēruchai*) liberty to the captives,
> and the opening of the prison to those who are bound;
> to proclaim (*kalesai*) the year of the Lord's favor.

Why does Jesus switch words when He says He's proclaiming the year of the Lord's favor? One theory is that Jesus took a homiletics course in seminary where He learned that repeating words makes you more rhetorically powerful. But there's a better theory, and it comes in two parts.

Part One begins with the observation that the *Hebrew* version of Isaiah 61:1 uses the same word both times. Here's how it reads:

> ... to proclaim (*liq'ro*) liberty to the captives,
> and the opening of the prison to those who are bound;
> to proclaim (*liq'ro*) the year of the Lord's favor.

By using the same word two times, Jesus is not departing from Isaiah; He's just participating in a different tradition of reading it. He restores a verbal parallel that already existed in the Hebrew Scriptures and which, for whatever reason, had been obscured in the LXX. What the Anointed One in the text proclaims, what the Melchizedekian figure proclaims, and what Jesus Himself proclaims in Galilee, is two-fold: it is a ministry program—*aphesis*, or "release"—and it is the dawning of a particular time—the "year of the Lord's favor."

This isn't itself a "Big Deal." It doesn't change the basic meaning of the words. English translations aren't hiding key, need-to-know claims about Jesus' ministry. But Luke's text has layers of meaning, and this is another example of the text using subtle word associations to develop those layers of meaning. It reinforces

SUNDAY

what the surface of the text has already made explicit: There's a meaningful relationship between "release" and "Jubilee." But it also encourages us to pay closer attention to Jesus' word choice.

Part Two, one reason why Isaiah uses the same word for proclaim—*liq'ro*, from the root, *qarah*—is that this was already a key Leviticus verb. The very first word of Leviticus is "And then he called" (from *qarah*, 1:1). Then it's the beginning of the calendar: "These are the appointed feasts of Yahweh that you shall proclaim (*qarah*) as holy convocations" (23:2, 4). It's also how the Jubilee was kicked off: On that day, "you shall consecrate the fiftieth year and proclaim (*qarah*) liberty throughout the land to all its inhabitants" (25:10).

In Leviticus, Yahweh calls to Israel (1:1), and He commissions Moses, their president, to proclaim both feasts (Lev 23) and pardons (Lev 25). So it makes sense that the Anointed One of Isaiah 61 is sent to "proclaim" (*qarah*) release to the captives and to "proclaim" (*qarah*) the Year of the Lord's favor.

The word *qarah* is by no means a rare one. It has its share of special uses, but most of its uses are common ones. For some reason, the LXX adds nuance where the Hebrew doesn't, translating the same word a whole bunch of different ways. At Leviticus 25:10, it uses *diaboēsete*. Then in Isaiah 61 it uses *kēruchai* and *kalesai*.

What the LXX *does* recognize is that the Year of Jubilee is about *aphesis*. Here's what it does with Leviticus 25:10–11:

> You shall consecrate the fiftieth year, and proclaim liberty (*aphesin*) throughout the land to all its inhabitants. It shall be a jubilee (*apheseōs*) for you, when each of you shall return to his property and each of you shall return to his clan. That fiftieth year shall be a jubilee (*apheseōs*) for you.

When Jesus proclaims *aphesis* to the captives (4:18), the fact that He's proclaiming "release" is literally on the surface. When Jesus proclaims the Year of the Lord's favor later on in the very same sentence (4:19), He's proclaiming "release" again, but just under the surface.

In conclusion, on the Sabbath, Jesus proclaims a Big Sabbath.

He draws from passages about the Sabbath Year (Isa 58) and the Year of Jubilee (Isa 61). He announces a ministry featuring *aphesis*/"release" and puts that theme right at the center. The rest of this chapter will simply argue that Jesus doesn't stop doing this and that His words and His works only reinforce His big view of the Sabbath.

Sabbatical Beatitudes

Most commentators agree that the single Old Testament passage that gives the most form to Luke's and Matthew's Beatitudes is Isaiah 61:1–3. And *we* already know that Isaiah 61:1–3 reflects a development of Sabbath and Jubilee traditions.

But before talking about Luke's development of Sabbath themes in his Beatitudes, it bears mentioning that the distinguishing feature of Luke's Beatitudes is their decidedly *material* focus. Take the first one. Where Matthew says, "Blessed are the poor *in spirit*, for theirs is the kingdom of heaven," Luke says, "Blessed are the poor," without qualification, and then makes essentially the same promise: "yours is the kingdom of God" (Matt 5:2; Luke 6:20). Luke's second Beatitude addresses "you who are hungry now," while Matthew's addresses "those who hunger and thirst *for righteousness*" (Luke 6:21a; Matt 5:6a). And both offer the same reward: "for you/they shall be satisfied" (Luke 6:21b; Matt 5:6b).

This focus of the text on the material poor is important because it harmonizes the Beatitudes according to the same key as Jesus' Big Sabbath proclamation described above. When Jesus says at 6:20 that the poor are blessed, this is simply a direct application of His ministry program: "to proclaim good news to the poor" (4:18; cf. Isa 61:1). The good news introduced at 4:18 is, as it turns out, that they are blessed and that theirs is the kingdom of God.

The Beatitudes also harmonize with Mary's song in 1:46–55. Mary had sung the words, "He has filled the hungry with good things, and the rich he has sent away empty" (1:53). Luke's second of three Beatitudes, and the "Woe" that goes with it, say the same thing: "Blessed are you who are hungry now, for you shall be satisfied.... Woe to you who are full now, for you shall be hungry" (6:21, 25).

Luke's third Beatitude does the same kind of thing. He addresses it to "those who weep now," and Isaiah talks about "those who mourn" two times in those verses (Luke 6:21; Isa 61:2–3). Isaiah promises them "comfort," "a beautiful headdress," and "the oil of gladness;" Jesus tells them that they "will laugh" (6:20).

Luke's Beatitudes *fill out* Jesus' Big Sabbath Proclamation and show His commitment to an Isaiah-61-themed ministry. He says He will bring good news to the poor, and then He does. He says that the hungry will be satisfied and that those who mourn will laugh. But His words about "love of enemies" in the next chapter are even *more* profoundly rooted in Sabbath themes.

Sabbatical Love of Enemies

In Matthew, Jesus follows His Beatitudes by responding to Old Testament teachings and rabbinic sayings with the words, "But I say to you." The point seems to have been to emphasize the "I" in "But I say to you" in order to emphasize His authority as a teacher.

In Luke, Jesus uses the same words, but He seems to emphasize the "you" part in order to emphasize the distinct character of the ministry of His disciples. "Even sinners lend to sinners," but Jesus' disciples will be different. Their love for their enemies will be characterized by three specific actions: "love," "do good," and "give" (*didōmi*). He describes these three actions in 6:27–31. He elaborates on the words "love" (v. 32) and "do good" (v. 33), and then He elaborates on the word "give" by replacing it with the word "lend" (*daneizō*, v. 34). And He concludes His teaching by sticking to His new list: "But *love* your enemies, and *do good*, and lend (*daneizō*), expecting nothing in return, and your reward will be great" (v. 35).

The notion of lending and expecting nothing in return is a Sabbath Year and Year of Jubilee concept. Look at this piece of Year of Jubilee legislation at Leviticus 25:35–38:

> If your brother becomes poor and cannot maintain himself with you, you shall support him as though he were a stranger and a sojourner, and he shall live with you. Take no interest from him or profit, but fear your God, that your brother may live beside you. You shall not lend him your money at interest, nor give him your food for profit. I am Yahweh your God, who brought you out of the land of Egypt to give you the land of Canaan, and to be your God.

The skeptical reader might say, "Not impressed. We don't need a quote from Leviticus or a theological reason to tell us that it's good to lend without expecting anything. And I can't imagine Jesus needed it either. I read that principle in *The Giving Tree* when I was six. Plus, that's just called altruism, and all cultures value that."

Fair. But, for one thing, *The Giving Tree* never promises that "your reward will be great" if you give without expecting return. And, for another, the skeptical reader hasn't gotten to the tasty part yet. Consider this piece of Sabbath Year legislation at Deuteronomy 15:7–11, paying attention to some of the words used in the LXX:

> If among you, one of your brothers should become poor … you shall not harden your heart or shut your hand against your poor brother, but you shall open your hand to him and lend (*daneizō*) him sufficient for his need, whatever it may be. Take care lest there be an unworthy thought in your heart and you say, "The seventh year, the year of release is near," and your eye look grudgingly on your poor brother, and you give him nothing, and he cry to Yahweh against you, and you be guilty of sin. You shall give (*didōmi*) to him freely, and your heart shall not be grudging when you give (*didōmi*) to him…. Therefore I command you, "You shall open wide your hand to your brother, to the needy and to the poor, in your land."

Here, Yahweh instructs Israel to make interest-free loans at *all* times, to cancel the principal on the loan in the Sabbath Year, and then to expect to be blessed (remember: "your reward will be

SUNDAY

great," Luke 6:35). Notice the instructions both to give (*didōmi*, 15:10) and to lend (*daneizō*, 15:8). In this passage, the words are used almost synonymously. What's remarkable is that Luke 6:34 is the only text in the entire New Testament that uses the "lending" verb, *daneizō*, which suggests an intentional echo of this Sabbath Year passage. More than that, though, Luke also includes this other word, *didōmi*, right alongside it: "give and lend." Luke 6:34–35 and Deuteronomy 15:7–11 are the only two texts in the entire Bible that use these terms together. Given Luke's love for these Big Sabbath texts, I am hardly surprised.

What does this mean? It means that when Jesus wants to teach His disciples about loving their enemies, He does it specifically by drawing from Sabbath ethics: In the kind of Jubilee that Jesus proclaims, the Sabbath legislation about lending freely to one's brother without grudging applies beyond the bonds of brotherhood. Keeping the Sabbath means extending "release" even to one's enemies.

Sabbatical Forgiveness

Jesus draws on the theme of "release" one more time in the next few verses. In vv. 37–38, He tells His disciples not only to "give, and [it] will be given to you," but also to "forgive, and you will be forgiven." In Deuteronomy 15, it was those who *gave* and *lent* without expectation of return who were to expect blessing. In Luke 6, it is also those who *forgive* without expectation of return during the Year of the Lord's favor who may expect blessing. We already knew that Jesus had a ministry of forgiveness, and it's not as if forgiveness was invented on the Sabbath. So what's the connection?

The first thing to notice is that the word translated "forgive" here is *apoluō*, which is more woodenly translated "release." I point this out because by this point, we know to pay attention to words that mean "release." That's not to say that *apoluō* doesn't also mean "forgive" and that English translators are mistaken for choosing the word "forgive" for *apoluō*. Forgiveness is *one kind* of release. But it *is* to say that this specific word brings up a very specific cluster of associations in Luke that usually pass right under our English-reading noses.

We think we know what forgiveness means.

Luke wants us to know that forgiveness is not a species of courtesy, and therefore a kind of etiquette, but a species of Sabbatical release, and therefore an ethical and sometimes *liturgical* reenactment of the Exodus.

Forgiveness is a release from the burden of debt and from the burden of guilt.

Simeon uses *apoluō* twice when he sings gratefully of being a bondservant "released" to "be released" in peace (2:29). Here, it doesn't mean "forgiven," but it takes that straightforward, manumissive sense. Simeon believes that the appearance of Jesus has released him from his service, into peace.

Jesus "releases" (*apoluō*) a man once He has exorcised him (8:38), He "releases" a crowd once He has taught them (9:12), He "releases" a woman once He has healed her of her disabling spirit (13:12), and then He "releases" a man once He heals him of his dropsy (14:4). The pattern couldn't be clearer: First, Jesus heals people, and then He "releases" them back into the world.

The other six times Luke uses *apoluō* in his Gospel are in chapter 23, when the people shout, "Release (*apoluō*) for us Barabbas!"

Those who know the story know that it's a tragic irony.

Barabbas kept company with rebels, being imprisoned along with those who had committed murder during the insurrections (23:19). On the surface, he profiles as a frustrated freedom fighter. Jesus may have become popular, but not popular enough.

The people show how "bound" they remained when they refuse to liberate their Liberator.

Then Luke uses *apoluō* fifteen more times in Acts: ten times to describe the "release" of prisoners, three times to describe disciples "released" for ministry assignments, and then two times more generally to describe the dismissal of an assembly.

So when Jesus tells His disciples "forgive, and you will be forgiven," the forgiveness He has in mind has something to do with Simeon's "release" unto peace and consolation, something

SUNDAY

to do with having been sent back into the world after having been healed, and something to do with being released from prison. All of these are part of Jesus' ministry of "release" in the Year of the Lord's favor. And forgiveness is not merely a moral value but a commemorative proclamation, an act of deliverance from oppression and captivity. Like the love of enemies, the proclamation of forgiveness, too, is grounded in Jesus' proclamation of the Big Sabbath. Keeping the Sabbath, and participating in Yahweh's rest, means proclaiming forgiveness.

Seven Sabbatical Works of "Release"

After telling the story of Jesus' Big Sabbath proclamation in 4:16–30, and before he gets to the Beatitudes, Enemy Love, and Forgiveness, Luke tells five stories of healings Jesus performs on the Sabbath in various parts of Galilee. Several chapters later, he tells two more Jesus-on-the-Sabbath stories. Five plus two. Count them: that's seven stories. I'll retell and comment on them in order:

First, on another Sabbath Day, this time in Capernaum, Jesus enters a synagogue and teaches (4:31–37). *What* Jesus teaches, Luke doesn't disclose. But whatever it is, is "astonishing" and possesses "authority." He follows His teaching by rebuking (*epitimaō*, 4:35) an unclean spirit, commanding it to come out of one of the men. Jesus had just said He was sent to release those who are oppressed (4:18), and the very next scene in Luke shows Him doing so. Not only is Jesus fulfilling the promises of His proclamation, but it's also specifically *on* the Sabbath that He fulfills them.

Second, leaving the synagogue that same Sabbath Day, He enters Simon's house and heals his mother-in-law (4:38–39). Just as He had rebuked (*epitimaō*, 4:35) the unclean spirit in the synagogue, He rebukes (*epitimaō*, 4:39) the fever that was constraining her. She is immediately healed and begins to serve them. After two stories, Luke is already establishing a pattern of Jesus rebuking invisible, oppressive forces on the Sabbath.

Does He sound like Melchizedek yet?

Third, on the same Sabbath, this time "when the sun was setting," Jesus does for the crowds what He had done earlier that day for the man and for Simon's mother: He drives out demons and heals diseases (4:40–41). For the third time in as many scenes, He rebukes (*epitimaō*, 4:41) the demons.

Either Luke is running out of material, or he's making a point. In either case, all he has to say is that, on the Sabbath, Jesus "rebukes" oppressive powers in order to heal and "release" people. And it's not a novel point: What Yahweh did to Pharaoh, Jesus is doing to these invisible forces of darkness.

By the time we get to the so-called "Sabbath controversies" in 6:1–5 and 6:6–11, it's no wonder the Pharisees are watching Him, "to see whether he would heal on the Sabbath" (6:7).

In these three stories, the pattern of healing by "rebuke" and "release" is the only constant. He heals men and women in the synagogue and in the home, from spiritual diseases and from physical ones, one-at-a-time and in large groups.

Fourth, Jesus feeds His disciples (6:1–5). Once the bare fact that "Jesus heals on the Sabbath" is no longer new or noteworthy, Luke tells a second triad of Sabbath stories featuring a new element: an articulate opposition. That's why these next three Sabbath stories have often been called "Sabbath controversies."

On a certain Sabbath Day, while He and His disciples are walking through a grain field, those disciples pick heads of grain to eat. Then a group of wild Pharisees appear, and they ask Him, "Why are you doing what is not lawful to do on the Sabbath?" (6:2) Jesus responds by asking them whether they've read about David and his companions unlawfully eating the bread of the presence when they were hungry. Readers are often tempted to think that the *gotcha!* moment in this story is when Jesus cites the example of David in 1 Samuel 21. Some of us are simply impressed that Jesus could remember a relevant Bible story under pressure. Others of us are curious about how and why Jesus decides to apply *this particular* story about David to Himself.

But that's not the point. Jesus wasn't the first rabbi to argue that it was permissible to prioritize "mercy" on the Sabbath. And not even all Pharisees held the same position! Jesus wasn't the first to cite David's story in a Sabbath debate. His answer was a conventional one; it was just a different convention from the one *these* Pharisees belonged to. The *gotcha!* moment actually comes later in the story.

According to the norms of *halakhic* debate, the structure and pacing of the conversation is unsurprising. The Pharisees were behaving normally by asking Jesus to explain His reasons for doing what He did on the Sabbath (6:2). Jesus was behaving normally by having responded with a citation from the Scriptures that supported His position (6:3–5). After this citation, the "defendant," Jesus, was supposed to offer a "ruling" or "statement of principle" based on the proof text they had chosen. And so when Mark tells this story, he includes one. In Mark's telling, Jesus follows up His citation of David's story by offering this statement of principle: "The Sabbath was made for man, and not man for the Sabbath" (Mark 2:27). Straightforward, true, and memorable.

Jesus was on His high school's debate team.

This "statement of principle" allows Mark to transition, nicely and neatly, into a concluding word about Jesus' authority over the Sabbath. Here's Mark's next sentence: "Therefore (*hōste*), the Son of Man is Lord even (*kai*) of the Sabbath" (2:28). Here is a summary of the flow of logic in Mark's telling of Jesus' response: "If we grant that we can categorize the Sabbath as one of those holy things that exists for the sake of man, it follows that it is one of those things that was made for the 'Son of Man,' too. And if the Son of Man has authority over those things that were made for man, it should come as no great surprise that the Son of Man has authority over the *Sabbath*, too, in addition to all of those other things."

But in Luke's telling, Jesus breaks the *halakhic* form. He never offers a "statement of principle" that the Sabbath was made for man. In fact, He doesn't say anything more about what the Sabbath is. He deletes the "therefore" (*hōste*) that Mark had used to show the logical transition between His argument and His claims about His authority. He deletes the word *kai*, which Mark had used to extend his application of the principle of Jesus' lordship—

3 SABBATH HERO

"The Son of Man is Lord"—to the case of the Sabbath—"Therefore, the Son of Man is Lord ... *even* of the Sabbath."

In most English translations, Luke's closing line reads, "The Son of Man is Lord of the Sabbath." But it's important to know that these translations get Luke's word order exactly backwards. In his own words, Luke says, *kurios estin tou sabbatou ho huios tou anthrōpou*. According to Luke's word order, here's how we should read it: "The Lord (*kurios*) of the Sabbath (*tou sabbatou*) is the Son (*huios*) of Man (*anthrōpou*)." On one level, this doesn't matter. This sounds like the "symmetric property" that students learn in sixth grade math: if $a = b$, then $b = a$. That allows us to flip sentences like these around and get the same meaning. The Son of Man *is* Lord of the Sabbath, and the Lord of the Sabbath *is* the Son of Man.

But, in this case, the word order matters for rhetorical reasons. When Jesus begins with the words, "The Lord of the Sabbath is ... ," everyone knows how that sentence is supposed to end: "Yahweh. The Lord of the Sabbath is Yahweh." *Yahweh* rested on the first seventh day. *Yahweh* delivered Israel from the tyrannical Pharaoh, who had usurped his lordship when he told Moses and Aaron that he would not release them for three days of rest, and then set up a weekly holiday to commemorate this deliverance. *Yahweh* is the one who said, "Above all, you shall keep *my* sabbaths," and then folded the Sabbath into Israel's manumission laws and their sevenly calendar. Pharaoh pretends to be Lord of the Sabbath, and so do all those who fail to release their households unto rest on the seventh day. The true Lord of the Sabbath is Yahweh.

In Luke, this is where Jesus steps out of line. He says, "The Lord of the Sabbath is...." Then His disciples pull out a snare drum and perform a drum roll. He pauses. Looks around at nervous faces. Sticks both His thumbs square in His chest. Finishes His sentence: "The Lord of the Sabbath is *the Son of Man*."

Gasp.

This is the *gotcha!* moment. Like Yahweh, Mattathias, and the mythical Melchizedek, Jesus had kept the Sabbath by "rebuking" oppressors and "releasing" or "setting at liberty" their captives. Jesus not only keeps the Sabbath Command in its fullest sense, but He claims for Himself a title that had, until this point, been reserved for Yahweh, the God of the Exodus. Jesus doesn't just claim to be the president in charge of proclaiming the Sabbath; He identifies Himself as The One who Says "Let My People Go." That's why they start discussing "what they might do to Jesus" (6:11).

This means that Jesus can say "my Sabbaths" (cf. Exod 31:13) the way Yahweh does, even as the Pharisees worry that *their own* Sabbath is being desecrated.

Fifth, "on another Sabbath," Jesus enters the synagogue with the purpose of teaching (6:6–11). While a cohort of scribes and Pharisees "watched him, to see whether He would heal on the Sabbath," He takes a break from teaching and calls up a man with a withered hand. He asks this group of Sabbath watchers the question that makes Him sound like David and Mattathias: "Is it lawful on the Sabbath to do good or to do harm, to save life or to destroy it?" Then Jesus restores the man's hand. Luke tells us that this "fills" (*plēthō*) the scribes and Pharisees with "rage" (*anoia*). Jesus is healing again, and Luke is dropping Easter eggs (Sabbath eggs?) in the corners of his stories. Here are a few:

To begin with, that Jesus "fills" people with "rage" should sound familiar. The only other time Jesus is said to have "filled" (*plēthō*) anyone with "rage" (*anoia*) is in 4:28, right after He finished proclaiming His Big Sabbath. That was *also* on a Sabbath and *also* in a synagogue. And it was right after He'd reminded the people that Elisha cleansed the leprosy of Naaman the Syrian. Just know, again, that Luke's seven Sabbath stories are connected, and Jesus' lordship of the Sabbath consistently infuriates synagogue attendees.

For another, these Pharisees and scribes don't just "watch" Jesus, but they "watch him closely" (*paratēreō*). This is another rare word in the New Testament, used only six times. Four of those uses are Luke's: the scribes and Pharisees watch Jesus closely to see if He will heal on the Sabbath (6:7); then they do it again (14:1; Mark uses *paratēreō* in a parallel story in 3:2); they watch closely

3 SABBATH HERO

for a reason to put Jesus to death a third time (20:20); and then Paul gets watched closely (Acts 9:24). The sixth use of *paratēreō* was probably the first one written down, and it comes in one of Paul's descriptions of the Galatians before they knew the freedom of the gospel:

> Formerly, when you did not know God, you were enslaved to those that by nature are not gods. But now that you have come to know God, or rather to be known by God, how can you turn back again to the weak and worthless elementary principles of the world, whose slaves you want to be once more? You observe (*paratēreō*) days and months and seasons and years! I am afraid I may have labored over you in vain. (4:8–11)

The ESV translates *paratēreō* "observe," but I don't think that's fair. At all six places in the New Testament, *paratēreō* refers to an overly-scrupulous vigilance, animated by the intention of finding fault with another person's behavior. "To observe," in English, has a positive, or even a neutral connotation. Abbott-Smith's gloss on the Greek word is straightforwardly negative: "to watch closely; observe narrowly with evil intent."[6] These words from Paul perfectly describe the party of scribes and Pharisees that comes to close-watch Jesus on the Sabbath. The irony is that those who are close-watching Jesus are slaves to not-gods, and so *they* are the ones who stand in need of Sabbath-day deliverance from their oppressors. This highlights the central irony of the Pharisees' observance of the Sabbath: They spend the weekly Day of Release willfully enslaving themselves to a spirit which binds them.

This also alters the sense of Galatians 4. The Galatians have not erred by observing "the Sabbath," as a concept. They have erred by keeping the Pharaonic Sabbath, the Pharisaical Sabbath, and, at worst, Mr. Covey's Christmas.

On the surface, Paul's final comment in this passage appears to be merely emotional: "I am afraid I may have labored over you in vain." But what Paul is actually doing is identifying his work

---

6. *A Manual Greek Lexicon of the New Testament,* ed. George Abbot-Smith, 6th ed. (London: T&T Clark, 2000), s.v. *"Paratēreō".*

SUNDAY

of Christian ministry—which he will compare to motherhood in the following verses—with God's work of creation in Genesis 1. If the Galatians remain overly scrupulous about keeping times and seasons, failing to keep the Sabbath of Jesus and walk in freedom, then his laborious work of creation has not succeeded. Yahweh creates, rests, and grants His creation a participation in His rest. Paul (co-)creates, rests, and calls his children to participation in his rest. Paul's labor and writing resembles Yahweh's work of creation in Genesis and redemption in Exodus, and Jesus' work of rebuke, release, and disputation in His Sabbath stories.

Back to the story.

The main development in Luke's story of Jesus' Sabbath-Day healing of the man with the withered hand has to do with the way that Jesus defends His healing ministry. His words seem exaggerated: "Is it lawful on the Sabbath to do good or to do harm, to save life or to destroy it?" The man's *hand* is withered. Is he really dying? Does healing his hand equal "saving life"? Does waiting until tomorrow to heal his hand count as "destroying life"?

In a sense.

An insight from Greco-Roman medical thought has helped readers understand Jesus' words a little better.[7] According to the categories natural to the medical thought of the day, a hand that was withered was not a *disabled* hand but a *dead* one. And to restore *one part* of a body from death to life meant to restore the whole body from death to life. Jesus will soon heal the centurion's nearly-dead slave (7:2–10) and command a widow's dead son to "wake up" (7:11–17). When He does, those are Examples Two and Three of the same kind of healing ministry: restoring the dead to life. So when Jesus tells John's disciples, "The blind receive their sight, the lame walk, lepers are cleansed, and the deaf hear, *the dead are raised up*, [and] the poor have good news preached to them" (7:22), He has all three of these men in view—hand guy, slave, and son.

---

7. See the discussion in Matthew Thiessen, *Jesus and the Forces of Death: The Gospels' Portrayal of Ritual Impurity within First-Century Judaism* (Grand Rapids: Baker, 2020), 162–71.

The point is not to exaggerate the man's deathiness, but to point out that, for Jesus and His contemporaries, death was a relatively broad category. And that Jesus associates what He calls His dead-raising ministry (7:22) with His ministry of healing on the Sabbath (6:6–11). One of the oppressors whom Jesus rebukes, and from whom He delivers people, is Death. And what does that make the Sabbath? Among other things, as it turns out, it is a great day for releasing people from Death.

Sixth, Jesus heals a woman in a synagogue (13:10–17). He tells her, at the decisive moment, that she is "released" (*apoluō*) from her disease. "Released," again, is like the manumission of a servant, like the unchaining of a literal prisoner, and like the forgiveness of sins. When Peter's mother-in-law has her illness rebuked on the Sabbath, she begins serving Jesus; when this woman is "released" from her unclean spirit on the Sabbath, she begins glorifying God.

The synagogue official is milder in his opposition to Jesus' healing than the scribes and the Pharisees, but he still puts his foot down. This official turns to the crowd and points his finger at those who are starting to figure out that Jesus is a synagogue-Sabbath-healer: "There are six days in which work ought to be done. Come on those days and be healed, and not on the Sabbath day." Implicitly, the point is that healing is a species of the genus of work, and so is making a trip to the synagogue to *get healed*. But the official's problem is no longer Jesus; it's the crowd. Crowds are coming to get healed, and they know that Jesus heals on the Sabbath.

This official sets Jesus up to set the people straight. He knows that Jesus loves the law, and he quotes part of the Decalogue's original Sabbath Command (Exod 20:8–11), expecting to call Jesus back to the true meaning of the Law. By way of reminder, this is the text from which the official is drawing:

> Remember the Sabbath day, to keep it holy. *Six days you shall labor, and do all your work, but the seventh day is a Sabbath to the Lord your God.* On it you shall not do any work, you, or your son, or your daughter, your male servant, or your female

servant, or your livestock, or the sojourner who is within your gates. *For in six days the Lord made heaven and earth, the sea, and all that is in them, and rested on the seventh day.* Therefore the Lord blessed the Sabbath day and made it holy.

But Jesus brings out the popular sense of the law, appealing to the crowd's own sense of kindness and generosity: "Does not each of you on the Sabbath untie (*luō*; the root of *apoluō*) his ox or his donkey from the manger and lead it away to water it?" Remembering that Sabbath rest is explicitly for "your livestock," Jesus points to the kind of "work" that is no more than "releasing" the living souls under one's care. And so, if it is right and good to fulfill the Sabbath Command by "releasing" one's *livestock* on the Sabbath, there is nothing wrong with "releasing" a bound woman: "Ought not this woman, a daughter of Abraham whom Satan bound for eighteen years, be loosed (*luō*) from this bond on the Sabbath day?"

On the surface, Jesus' comparison appears demeaning: We "untie" oxen and donkeys. The fact that Jesus refers to donkeys and women as species of the same class can be head-scratching. But that's not what Jesus is getting at. What Jesus is getting at is the responsibility of the head of a household to care for the living souls (*nephesh*) under his roof. Any good man keeps the Sabbath by caring for his "livestock" and allowing them to rest, but Jesus keeps the Sabbath by identifying this woman as a "daughter" or a "female servant" of His household, and therefore as one to whom He owes a Sabbatical responsibility. And He cares for her as such.

Where the ruler sees "work" and Sabbath-breaking, Jesus sees "release unto rest" and Sabbath-keeping. How typical it is of those in positions of institutional power to reduce the point of the Sabbath to the general principle of "rest," when the weightier matter of the law—justice and mercy and faith—is "release" realized through the "rebuke" of the powers. Unlike the synagogue official, Jesus fulfills Parts One and Two of the Sabbath law.

Seventh, Jesus heals a man with dropsy (14:1–6). What makes this story so great is how predictable the Sabbath stories have become. Jesus goes to dine in the home of one of the leaders of the

3 SABBATH HERO

Pharisees, and they "watch him carefully" (*paratēreō*). Seen that one before. This time Jesus asks the question, "Is it lawful to heal on the Sabbath, or not?" and they have no answer. With no further ceremony, Jesus takes the man, heals him, and releases him (*apoluō*). Then Jesus brings the Sabbath question home, reinforcing the connection He'd made in the last story between livestock and children: "Which of you, having a son or an ox that has fallen into a well on a Sabbath day, will not immediately pull him out?" Again, the Pharisees make no answer.

In this seventh Sabbath story, it appears the Pharisees have finally and ironically rested from their labor of disputing the Law with Jesus.

Jesus is Lord of the Sabbath, the Yahweh-of-the-Exodus-become-flesh, Head of the Household of the World, Sabbath-Keeper *par excellence*. He sees every man and woman who approaches Him for healing as His son or His daughter, His male servant or female servant, and He keeps the Sabbath by "rebuking" their oppressors and "releasing" them unto their "rest." He loves His neighbor as Himself by keeping the Sabbath. He is Melchizedek, leader of a heavenly army of angels and disciples, authorized to carry out a Sabbatical campaign of *aphesis* in the Year of the Lord's Favor.

The purpose of this book is not, ultimately, to explain what the Sabbath is or how to keep it, but to make an argument for what Sunday means. What Sunday means *includes* the Sabbath, and it means at least as much. Luke shows us that Jesus fulfills the Sabbath Law neither by canceling its demands nor by avoiding them, but by taking upon Himself responsibility for the rebuke of the powers and the release of His children.

We keep the Sabbath on Sundays by commemorating that Jesus rebuked the powers of Sin and Death and proclaimed to us our release from the kingdom of darkness. Presidents in the Church are charged with the duty of festal speech, of keeping the Sabbath on Sundays by inviting us to confess our sins and by proclaiming Yahweh's absolution over us.

We keep the Sabbath by reading and by playing soccer in the

park. We keep the Sabbath by identifying the masters we used to serve and saying "No" to them, and we keep the Sabbath by abstaining from sin. We try not to check our work email. But if we do, it's because we want to and not because someone makes us.

We keep the Sabbath every day by loving our enemies, by forgiving one another, and by making our tithes and our loans according to our means and then sometimes going beyond them. The Sabbath is the shape of our whole life, and the Day is a concentrated commemoration and celebration of that life.

Excursus: Christ's Sabbatical Descensus

According to the Apostles' Creed, Jesus "descended to the dead" or "descended to Hell," depending how you're inclined to translate *descensus ad inferos*. And according to the Bible, He "descended to Sheol" or "Hades." Whatever this place that is named in the Scriptures and the Creed *is*, this is where Jesus spent the day that Israel would have called "the seventh day of the Feast of Unleavened bread, a solemn Sabbath" (Lev 23:8) and that the Church now calls "Holy Saturday."

What Jesus *did* "down there" is inferred from a number of Bible passages. In one place, Peter says, "he went and proclaimed to the spirits in prison" (1 Pet 3:18). In another, he says, "the gospel was preached even to the dead" (4:6). At Ephesians 4:8, Paul quotes Psalm 68, which says, "When he ascended on high, he led a host of captives," and then explains that this implies that He "descended into the lower regions of the earth." Different traditions have parsed out the location, actions, audience, and accomplishments of Jesus' *descensus* in different ways, emphasizing different texts and linking them to different doctrines.

Taking their cue from texts such as these, some sermons from the Fathers and some imaginative literature from the Medieval Church describe Jesus' actions on Holy Saturday as "The Harrowing of Hell." Essentially, this tradition understands Jesus as personally entering the habitation of those who have died and there performing some act of proclamation and *aphesis*. The Roman Catholic Catechism explains that Jesus opened the gates for those

3 SABBATH HERO

who died in faith, making possible their long-awaited entry into heaven. Eastern Orthodox iconography depicts a triumphant Jesus, standing on the broken gates of Hell and holding the hands of Adam and Eve, with the Devil bound in chains beneath them. Calvin understands Saturday as an extension of Jesus' suffering on Friday.[8] Luther understands Saturday as the prologue of Jesus' resurrection and ascension on Sunday.[9]

What I propose is neither an exegetical solution nor a doctrinal clarification, but an imaginative kernel. The text of Scripture makes three things indisputably clear: One, Jesus descended on the Sabbath. Two, He proclaimed something to some people. Three, He engaged in some kind of binding and loosing.

Here is what I see. I've written a chapter about how Jesus keeps the Sabbath, and when I see "Sabbath," "proclamation," and "binding and loosing," what am I supposed to imagine Jesus as having done? The "Collect for Holy Saturday" in the Book of Common Prayer says that Jesus "was laid in the tomb and rested on this holy Sabbath." But neither Luke nor the Apostles' Creed have given us any stories that would suggest to us that Jesus did anything other than what He always seemed to be doing on the Sabbath: rebuking oppressors, proclaiming liberty to captives, and releasing them unto their rest. Perhaps Jesus rested. Perhaps He continued dethroning the powers and proclaiming liberty to the children of God. More than probably, the mystery of God in Christ is that those two actions—rest and the evangelical proclamation of release—are one and the same thing.

---

8. John Calvin, *The Institutes of the Christian Religion*, ed. John T. McNeill, trans. Ford Lewis Battles, 2 vols. (Philadelphia: Westminster, 1960), II.XVI.11.

9. Martin Luther, "The Third Sermon, on Easter Day," trans. Jayson S. Galler and Susanne Hafner, *Logia 12*, no. 3 (2003): 37–50.

4 PASSOVER PRESIDENT

"Your new moons and your appointed feasts my soul hates."

Isaiah 1:14

"In every generation, each person must say: 'This which the Lord did for me,' and not: 'This which the Lord did for my forefathers.'"

Pesachim 116b:3 on Exodus 13:8

When the Scripture tells the story of the Passover in Exodus 12, its primary focus is to instruct Israel how to ritually commemorate that night (vv. 1–25) and how to explain those ritual elements to children (vv. 26–27). The actual "story" of the Passover itself follows in five short verses (vv. 28–32).

Yahweh intended that all Israel ritually remember, at the beginning of each year, that their national story begins with Yahweh's overthrow of Pharaoh and his armies, and that He delivered them from out of Pharaoh's house of slavery. If the Sabbath

4 PASSOVER PRESIDENT

holiday means "rest for the whole household," the Passover holiday means "deliverance for the whole nation." The commemorative rite involves blood as a ritual sign, the ritual consumption of unleavened bread, and the corporate consumption of an unblemished male lamb.

For the Church, Sunday is not just a Sabbath, but a weekly Passover. And while we remember and celebrate that Yahweh delivered Israel from Egypt, the heart of our remembrance and celebration is that Yahweh overthrew the powers of Sin and Death and their armies and that He delivered a new Israel, the Church, from the kingdom of darkness. The Church's ritual commemoration likewise consists of bread and wine, which are also, mysteriously, Christ's own flesh and blood. The Church is a holy nation and the city of God, and this story of Christ's Passover and our deliverance is the beginning of our civic history.

That Jesus celebrates the Passover surprises no one. Israelite men had presided over Passover celebrations every year since Moses. Jesus must have inherited local traditions for keeping the weeklong "Feast of Unleavened Bread" from His neighborhood, not unlike the way kids grow up learning how their churches celebrate Christmas.

When Jesus celebrates the Passover and uses the night as an occasion to institute a new commemorative rite, He doesn't forget all the stories. He remembers, and He fulfills, all of the great Passover traditions from Israel's national history. He knew Exodus 12, but He also knew the stories of Moses' Passover celebration at Sinai and Joshua's in Canaan, the celebrations of Kings Josiah and Hezekiah, and the one at the consecration of the new temple by Ezra's Levites. Each of these celebration stories repeats and develops the theme of "national deliverance," but in a new way. The Passover is a recurring feast that accumulates meaning over history. By the time it's Jesus' turn to celebrate it, the Passover is "full" (Gal 4:4) of meaning. We often remember that Jesus fulfills the role of "Passover lamb" (1 Cor 5:7), but He *also* fulfills the role of "Passover president."

The Passover means "national deliverance," but all the texture of that meaning comes from the stories of Passovers past elsewhere in the Bible. The meaning of Passover isn't a secret or an esoteric doctrine. It's not hidden under the surface of passages in Exodus or Leviticus, and it's not tucked away in extra-biblical documents. It's on the surface of the underappreciated texts that tell the stories of Passovers past. This chapter will retell those stories and show that Jesus' Passover celebration keeps all of them alive.

Passover Expectation

During "Passover time," Yahweh does Passover things.

In Chapter 2, I quoted this line from time scholar Sacha Stern: "particular days of the calendar, especially festival and fast days, are designated for the historical or eschatological recurrence of analogous events." When a biblical author frames a story as happening during the Passover, he expects us to relate it to the Passover stories that come before it.

Luke tells three "Passover stories."

His first one begins at Luke 2:41–42. "Now his parents went to Jerusalem every year at the Feast of the Passover. And when he was twelve years old, they went up according to custom." If the reader knows her history and her calendar, this is where she pulls the book up closer to her nose and asks "and *then* what did Yahweh do?"

His second one begins at Luke 22:1. "Now the Feast of Unleavened Bread drew near, which is called the Passover." Sharp inhale. Things happen. Then he circles closer. "Then came the day of Unleavened Bread, on which the Passover lamb had to be sacrificed" (22:7). Sharp inhale. Like Exodus 12, instructions are given and followed. Then he circles closer. "And when *the hour came*" (22:14). Now the reader expects a "historical and eschatological recurrence" of an event analogous to the original Passover.

His third one begins in Acts 12. "Herod the king laid violent hands on some who belonged to the church. He killed James the brother of John with the sword, and when he saw that it pleased the Jews, he proceeded to arrest Peter also" (12:1–3a). The episode sounds utterly bleak until Luke makes his winking,

4 PASSOVER PRESIDENT

"oh-by-the-way" comment: "This was during the days of Unleavened Bread" (12:3b).

Okay, well now we all feel better. Sure, Herod delivers Peter over to "four squads of soldiers," and he intends "after the Passover to bring him out to the people" (12:4). But Herod is the fool for waiting until after the Passover. Peter is the rock upon whom Christ will build His Church. Did he expect Yahweh to spend Passover *not* delivering him from prison? The story continues: "earnest prayer for him was made to God by the church" (12:5). Luke's readers remember that Israel cried out to God for rescue from slavery (Exod 2:35), and they know what Yahweh's going to do for Peter.

The story of "Peter's Passover" contains a couple of other Passover-themed Easter eggs. Here is how the story reads:

> Now when Herod was about to bring him out, *on that very night*, Peter was sleeping between two soldiers, bound with two chains, and sentries before the door were guarding the prison. And behold, an angel of the Lord stood next to him, and a light shone in the cell. He struck Peter on the side and woke him, saying, "*Get up quickly*." And the chains fell off his hands. And the angel said to him, "Dress yourself and *put on your sandals*." And he did so. And he said to him, "Wrap your cloak around you and follow me." And he went out and followed him. He did not know that what was being done by the angel was real, but thought he was seeing a vision. When they had passed the first and the second guard, they came to the iron gate leading into the city. It opened for them of its own accord, and they went out and went along one street, and immediately the angel left him. When Peter came to himself, he said, "Now I am sure that the Lord has sent his angel and rescued me from the hand of Herod and from all that the Jewish people were expecting." (vv. 6–12)

In Exodus 12, Yahweh instructs Moses and Aaron to "put on their sandals" and "move quickly" (v. 11). In Acts 12, the angel instructs Peter to "put on his sandals" and "move quickly" (vv. 7–8). And in both stories, an angel leads captive(s) out at nighttime.

That Yahweh accomplishes Peter's deliverance on "that very night" is Luke's subtlest nod to the Exodus. You wouldn't think it,

SUNDAY

but the phrase "that night" or "that very night" is actually a rare one. Jesus uses it twice to talk about the night He will be betrayed (Matt 26:34; Mark 14:30), which occurs during Passover. He uses it again to talk about the night He will return (Luke 17:34), which we will see later in this chapter is also like the Passover.

"That night" is a liturgical shorthand for the Passover. Or so a few scholars have argued.[1] Most of the biblical evidence comes from a series of "day" and "night" phrases in Exodus 12–13. Here they are: "I will pass through the land of Egypt *that night*" (12:12); "*this day* shall be for you a memorial day" (12:14); "*on this very day* I brought your hosts out of the land of Egypt" (12:17a); "therefore you shall observe *this day*" (12:17b); "at the end of 430 years, on *that very day*, all the hosts of Yahweh went out" (12:41); "it was *a night* of watching by Yahweh" (12:42a); "so this same night is a night of watching kept to Yahweh by all the people of Israel throughout their generations" (12:42b); "*on that very day* Yahweh brought the people of Israel out of the land of Egypt" (12:51); "remember *this day* in which you came out from Egypt" (13:3); "*today*, in the month of Abib, you are going out" (13:4).

When Luke begins the story of Peter's Passover by saying that "on that very night" Peter was sleeping, after having already thrown in a parenthetical comment about it being Passover time, we're ready for a Passover story. When Luke tells a Passover story, he wants his readers to think Exodus thoughts.

That remains true when we consider Luke's *first* Passover story:

> Now his parents *went to Jerusalem* every year at the Feast of the Passover. And when he was twelve years old, they went up according to custom. And when the feast was ended, as they were returning, the boy Jesus stayed behind in Jerusalem. His parents did not know it, but supposing him to be in the group they went a day's journey, but then they *began to search for him* among their relatives and acquaintances, and when they did

---

1. See, for example, J. Duncan M. Derrett, "'On That Night': Luke 17:34," *Evangelical Quarterly* 68 (1996): 38; Dany Christopher, *The Appropriation of Passover in Luke-Acts* (Tübingen: Mohr-Siebeck, 2018).

not find him, they returned to Jerusalem, *searching for him. After three days* they found him in the temple, sitting among the teachers, listening to them and asking them questions. *And all who heard him were amazed at his understanding and his answers.* And when his parents saw him, they were astonished. And his mother said to him, "Son, why have you treated us so? Behold, your father and I have been *searching for you* in great distress." And he said to them, "Why were you looking for me? Did you not know that I must be in my Father's house?" And they *did not understand* (*suniēmi*) the saying that he spoke to them. And he went down with them and came to Nazareth and was submissive to them. And his mother treasured up all these things in her heart. (Luke 2:41–51)

Well, Peter's Passover sounded a lot like an exodus. We had Passover time, the prayers of the people, "that night," getting up quickly, putting on sandals, the theme of release from captivity, and the leadership of an angel. There's no question that Peter's is a Passover story.

This story in Luke 2 doesn't sound so obviously like an exodus. So what's going on?

What is interesting about this story is how closely it matches up not with the *exodus*, but with Jesus' Passover-time Passion in Luke 22. A few observations:

First, this episode occurs at the end of Jesus' family's journey to Jerusalem. Jesus journeys to Jerusalem only two times in Luke. Here, at Passover. And then, famously, He starts His major journey to Jerusalem at 9:51, where He won't arrive until just before the Passover in 19:41. The point is, both times Jesus arrives in Jerusalem, it's Passover time, and Luke has an important story to tell.

Second, this is only one of two moments in Luke where Jesus is teaching in the temple. Notice that everyone there is amazed at Jesus' understanding and His answers, and it's no surprise that Jesus fits in really well, both with these people and in this setting. He even tells His parents that they shouldn't have been surprised to find Him here. One reason is that He's in His element. Jesus, however, won't teach in the temple again until right before

SUNDAY

Passover, in chapters 19–21. If you lived anywhere near Jerusalem, you would have had to have kicked yourself for missing it. Jesus only offered two postgraduate Bible seminars there. Both of them were right before Passover, and they were about twenty years apart. In the words of one commentator, Jesus' amazing and enigmatic words in Luke 2 "anticipate his final teaching in the temple at Passover time during Passion week."[2]

Third, Luke mentions three times that Jesus' parents "search" for Him, implying that He is lost (2:44, 45, 49). Readers of Luke will remember that Luke only tells one other story about a lost son—the prodigal son. That son is first described as "dead" and then "alive again" (15:24), and then immediately, as "lost" and then "found" (vv. 24, 32). This suggests that, for Luke, a "lost son" implies a "dead son," and the fact that Jesus is "found," and especially that He is found "after three days" has everyone who knows the *end* of Luke's Gospel thinking resurrection thoughts. Twice, around Passover, Jesus is lost for three days, and then found. The icing on the cake is that Jesus rhetorically asks His parents why they were looking for Him (2:49) just as the angel rhetorically asks the women why they were looking for the living among the dead (24:5).

Fourth, Jesus' parents "did not understand" (*suniēmi*) what He told them (2:50). Luke has other words he likes to use to talk about "understanding," but he saves this one for special moments. Here, for one. Then again at 8:10 to explain to His disciples that other people don't understand the mysteries of the kingdom of God because that knowledge is hidden from them. And then in this very interesting way at 18:34:

> And taking the twelve, he said to them, "See, we are going up to Jerusalem, and everything that is written about the Son of Man by the prophets will be accomplished. For he will be delivered over to the Gentiles and will be mocked and shamefully treated and spit upon. And after flogging him, they will kill him, and on the third day he will rise." But they understood (*suniēmi*) none

---

2. Craig A. Evans, *Luke*, NIBC (Peabody: Hendrickson, 1995), 42.

4 PASSOVER PRESIDENT

of these things. This saying was hidden from them, and they did not grasp what was said. (Luke 18:31–34)

Once again, Jesus says that a mystery is hidden. And just as at 2:50, it's in the context of a death that comes before a third day resurrection. The disciples don't understand until the third day, when the resurrected Jesus finally explains how the Scriptures prefigure His Passover-time Passion, and He *makes* them understand (*suniēmi*) Him (24:45). That's Luke's fourth and final use of the word. It seems that Luke saves *suniēmi* to signify the understanding of the mysteries of God at work in the death and resurrection of Jesus.

Luke tells the story of Peter's Passover (Acts 12:1–19) to recall the Exodus. He tells the story of Young Jesus in the Temple (Luke 2:41–52) to connect the Passover to the Passion. Not because the two *needed* to be so thickly connected, but because Luke likes laying it on thick.

And it gets even thicker.

Luke spends the whole dramatic thrust of his Gospel making his audience bounce up and down in their chairs expecting a major Passover event in the closing chapters. One scholar has assembled a list of seven (!) successive signs:[3]

One, Moses and Elijah speak to Jesus about His "exodus" (Greek: *exodos*), which He was about to accomplish at Jerusalem (9:30–31). Think about it. Some people use the word "exodus" without fully appreciating what that word means. But who knows what the word *exodos* means better than Moses? When Luke tells you a story where Moses—literally *Moses*—is standing around asking Jesus about His exodus, you know something big is going to happen.

Two, immediately, Jesus sets His face toward Jerusalem, and He never looks back (9:51). All of a sudden, this is important, because we know that Jesus is setting His GPS to Jerusalem in order to do an Exodus. And His ETA is "Passover time."

---

3. For detailed scholarly discussions of some of the passages in this chapter, see Christopher, *Appropriation of Passover*.

SUNDAY

Three, just before Jesus arrives in Jerusalem, and just before the Passover, the Pharisees ask when the kingdom of God is going to come (17:20–21). They want to know if *this* Passover is *the* Passover when Israel will be delivered from their oppressors.

Four, the Pharisees ask *When?* Then the disciples ask *Where?* (17:37).

Five, when Jesus finally arrives in Jerusalem, the crowd behaves as if the kingdom of God is about two minutes away: "As they heard these things, he proceeded to tell a parable, because *he was near to Jerusalem*, and because *they supposed that the kingdom of God was to appear immediately*" (19:11).

Six, after telling His parable, He approaches Jerusalem, mounts a donkey, and enters the city to shouts of, "Blessed is the King who comes in the name of the Lord! Peace in heaven and glory in the highest!" (19:28–40).

Seven, then Luke slowly approaches the big Passover story in those three stages: "Now the Feast of Unleavened Bread drew near, which is called the Passover ..." (22:1). "Then came the day of Unleavened Bread, on which the Passover lamb had to be sacrificed ..." (22:7). "And when *the hour came*"! (22:14).

That's when Jesus, the Passover President, takes the Passover Cup and the Passover Bread and opens His mouth ...

Passover History

... just like many great men of Israel before Him. When Jesus lifts the Bread and the Cup, these are the sandals He fills. Jesus' Passover celebration fulfills each of these historical celebration stories that He grew up reading.

The first Passover story was Moses' (Num 9:1–14). Pay attention to the care the text pays to the *timing* of the commemoration, the issue that the timing raises, and the way that Yahweh deals with that issue.

> And Yahweh spoke to Moses in the wilderness of Sinai, in the first month of the second year after they had come out of the land of Egypt, saying, "Let the people of Israel keep the Passover

4 PASSOVER PRESIDENT

at its appointed time. On the fourteenth day of this month, at twilight, you shall keep it at its appointed time; according to all its statutes and all its rules you shall keep it." So Moses told the people of Israel that they should keep the Passover. And they kept the Passover in the first month, on the fourteenth day of the month, at twilight, in the wilderness of Sinai; according to all that Yahweh commanded Moses, so the people of Israel did. And there were certain men who were unclean through touching a dead body, so that they could not keep the Passover on that day, and they came before Moses and Aaron on that day. And those men said to him, "We are unclean through touching a dead body. Why are we kept from bringing Yahweh's offering at its appointed time among the people of Israel?" And Moses said to them, "Wait, that I may hear what Yahweh will command concerning you."

Yahweh spoke to Moses, saying, "Speak to the people of Israel, saying, If any one of you or of your descendants is unclean through touching a dead body, or is on a long journey, he shall still keep the Passover to Yahweh. *In the second month on the fourteenth day at twilight* they shall keep it. They shall eat it with unleavened bread and bitter herbs. They shall leave none of it until the morning, nor break any of its bones; according to all the statute for the Passover they shall keep it. But if anyone who is clean and is not on a journey fails to keep the Passover, that person shall be cut off from his people because he did not bring Yahweh's offering *at its appointed time*; that man shall bear his sin. And if a stranger sojourns among you and would keep the Passover to Yahweh, according to the statute of the Passover and according to its rule, so shall he do. You shall have one statute, both for the sojourner and for the native."

The first thing to say about "timing" is that timing matters tremendously to Yahweh. He uses the phrase "at its appointed time" four separate times. Then, in the opening line of the story, the text dates the Passover in relation to the Exodus. He follows this by introducing the appointed time in a concentric triad of times. When? The first month. When? The fourteenth day. When? At twilight. Finally, the reason the first Passover "controversy"

SUNDAY

happens at all is because everyone knows the "appointed time" matters so much to Yahweh. Those who were unclean that day didn't have the gall to celebrate late without first asking Moses, and Moses didn't have the gall to make a rescheduling decision without asking Yahweh. The "Backup Passover" simulates that precise moment as well as possible. It still has to be on the fourteenth day at twilight, but the second month will have to do for these folks who are unclean.

But the most interesting thing about the timing of Moses' Passover is what happens next. Israel sets out from the wilderness of Sinai "in the second year, in the second month, on the twentieth day of the month" (10:11). Backup Passover was in Year 2, Month 2, Day 14. Add one more week for the Backup Feast of Unleavened Bread, which would have immediately followed (Lev 23:4–8), and you see that their departure date, Year 2, Month 2, Day 20, follows on the seventh day of their backup celebrations. Why is it so important that *all* Israel, clean and unclean, sojourner and native, celebrate the Passover that year? Lots of reasons. But the biggest one may have been that they were all setting off on their journey the very next day.

This illustrates the liturgical principle embedded in Israel's Passover: "in every generation a person must see himself as if he has [just] come out of Egypt." Moses celebrates the Passover because Israel needs to imagine that they are heading straight from Egypt into the wilderness of Paran. The liturgical effect of the Passover is that it abridges history. To the objective journalist, Israel had been out of Egypt for nearly fourteen months. But in the liturgical memory of the people, which means more, they'd all just left Egypt the night before.

The second Passover story is Joshua's (5:10–12), and the planning for the celebration seems uneventful. The text is short. The first half focuses on the setting, including the timing; the second half talks about what follows it:

> While the people of Israel were encamped at Gilgal, they kept the Passover *on the fourteenth day of the month in the evening* on the plains of Jericho. And the day after the Passover, *on that*

4 PASSOVER PRESIDENT

very day, they ate of the produce of the land, unleavened cakes and parched grain. And the manna ceased the day after they ate the produce of the land. And there was no longer manna for the people of Israel, but they ate of the fruit of the land of Canaan that year.

The day after the Passover in Exodus 12, Israel left Egypt. The day after Moses' Passover in Numbers 9–10, Israel set out for the wilderness of Paran. The day after *Joshua's* Passover, Israel starts to eat the fruit of Canaan. Passover matters, but the text teaches us that so does the day right after Passover.

Again, the point is that Israel's liturgical calendar, and especially the Passover, abridges their history. The effect of Joshua's Passover is that, again, every member of the new generation may "see himself as if he has [just] come out of Egypt." Even though the Exodus was technically forty years ago, and many of the people hadn't yet been born, this liturgical commemoration communicates that all Israel was in Egypt just last night and that today they're eating the fruit of Canaan. New food means a new nation. That's why, immediately beforehand, Joshua circumcises them, "to roll away the reproach of Egypt" (5:9). That's also why, back in Leviticus 23, the Feast of Unleavened Bread (vv. 4–8), which includes the Passover, is directly followed by Firstfruits (vv. 9–14). Liturgically speaking, it is a quick walk from Egypt to Canaan; from slavery to settlement; from unleavened bread and bitter herbs to the firstfruits of a new world.

In each of these first three Passover stories (Exod 12; Num 9; Josh 5), Scripture records a Passover story the night before Israel experiences a meaningful change in their relationship to the land. The day after the Exodus, they leave the land of Egypt. The day after Moses' Passover, they leave Sinai for Paran. The day after Joshua's Passover, the manna's gone, and they begin harvesting. Fast-forwarding to Hezekiah and Josiah, it's right before the land is purged of idols. For Ezra, it's right before a national life centered around a new temple commences.

Luke presents us with Jesus celebrating a Passover the night before something big happens. This should make his readers wonder how Israel's relationship with the land is going to change in the next few days after the Last Supper.

The third Passover story is Hezekiah's (2 Chron 30:1–27). He's one of the few "good kings" and the first "good king" mentioned in 2 Chronicles. The first two things the Chronicler tells us about Hezekiah's reign are that he repaired the temple (29:3–19) and restored its liturgical service (29:20–36). The only problem with this great undertaking is that it took too long: "They began to consecrate [the temple and themselves] on the first day of the first month, and on the eighth day of the month they came to the vestibule of Yahweh. Then for eight days they consecrated the house of Yahweh, and on the sixteenth day of the first month they finished" (29:17). If you noticed that this cut into Passover and the Feast of Unleavened Bread by two or three days, good for you. Many of these Israelites might not have caught that.

The next episode in Hezekiah's story is his broad and unifying summons to a Passover feast. "Better late than never," thought Hezekiah, like Moses. Here's what happens first:

> Hezekiah sent to all Israel and Judah, and wrote letters also to Ephraim and Manasseh, that they should come to the house of Yahweh at Jerusalem to keep the Passover to Yahweh, the God of Israel. For the king and his princes and all the assembly in Jerusalem had taken counsel to keep the Passover *in the second month*—for they could not keep it at that time because the priests had not consecrated themselves in sufficient number, nor had the people assembled in Jerusalem—and the plan seemed right to the king and all the assembly. (30:1–4)

Jehoshaphat had reached out to Ephraim at one point (19:4), and conducted some reforms in Judah (19:8) after the untimely death of their king, but no other Judean king in the books of Chronicles reaches out to *both* his own people in Judah *and* the kingdom of Israel. Hezekiah's invitation is an unprecedented gesture of pardon and unity in the era of the divided kingdom. And it goes better than anyone could have imagined:

4 PASSOVER PRESIDENT

Couriers went from city to city through the country of Ephraim and Manasseh, and as far as Zebulun, but they laughed them to scorn and mocked them. However, some men of Asher, of Manasseh, and of Zebulun humbled themselves and came to Jerusalem. The hand of God was also on Judah to give them one heart to do what the king and the princes commanded by the word of Yahweh. And many people came together in Jerusalem to keep the Feast of Unleavened Bread in the second month, a very great assembly. (30:10–13)

Everyone who had gathered in Jerusalem was willing, but not all of them were clean:

There were many in the assembly who had not consecrated themselves. Therefore the Levites had to slaughter the Passover lamb for everyone who was not clean, to consecrate it to Yahweh. For a majority of the people, many of them from Ephraim, Manasseh, Issachar, and Zebulun, had not cleansed themselves, yet they ate the Passover otherwise than as prescribed. (vv. 17–18)

Is this disobedient? No. The text goes on to assure us that Hezekiah had already prayed for a special dispensation, asking Yahweh's pardon on "everyone who sets his heart to seek God, Yahweh, the God of his fathers, even though not according to the sanctuary's rules of cleanness" (v. 19).

And the celebration is literally legendary. After keeping the Feast of Unleavened Bread for "seven days with great gladness,"

The whole assembly agreed together to keep the feast for another seven days. So they kept it for another seven days with gladness.... The whole assembly of Judah, and the priests and the Levites, and the whole assembly that came out of Israel, and the sojourners who came out of the land of Israel, and the sojourners who lived in Judah, rejoiced. So there was great joy in Jerusalem, for since the time of Solomon the son of David king of Israel there had been nothing like this in Jerusalem. (vv. 23, 25–26)

Once again, the Passover story doesn't end when the feast ends. What happens the next day matters:

SUNDAY

> Now when all this was finished, all Israel who were present went out to the cities of Judah and broke in pieces the pillars and cut down the Asherim and broke down the high places and the altars throughout all Judah and Benjamin, and in Ephraim and Manasseh, until they had destroyed them all. Then all the people of Israel returned to their cities, every man to his possession.... After these things and these acts of faithfulness, Sennacherib king of Assyria came and invaded Judah and encamped against the fortified cities, thinking to win them for himself. (31:1; 32:1)

Then the Chronicler includes Sennacherib's taunt of Judah because Sennacherib spoke better than he knew:

> Has not ... Hezekiah taken away his high places and his altars and commanded Judah and Jerusalem, "Before one altar you shall worship, and on it you shall burn your sacrifices"? (32:12)

Sennacherib goes on to use the word "deliver" eight times in a speech mocking Judah for believing that Yahweh would deliver them.

What all Judah knew, Sennacherib, like Herod, did not know: Yahweh delivers His people during Passover time. So no faithful reader is surprised by what Yahweh does next: "Yahweh sent an angel, who cut off all the mighty warriors and commanders and officers in the camp of the king of Assyria" (32:20). Yahweh, the great Catechist of His people, rewards His people for keeping *His* Passover by acting according to the pattern of the deeds He performed in Egypt.

Hezekiah's Passover story is the stuff of legend: the fourteen-day feast of gladness and joy, the sincerity of heart that was reckoned as ceremonial cleanliness, the gifts of reunion and one-heartedness, the every-man tirade against Judah's idols, and the war with Assyria that took one sentence to tell.

As American presidents have progressively realized their nation's aspirational value of Liberty in a distinctly American way, Yahweh and His presidents again realize the motif of deliverance in a distinctly Israelite way: Deliverance includes deliverance from the spirit of division, joyful participation in rites of commemoration, and the renewal of right worship in the land. The story of Hezekiah's Passover is the fruit of Hezekiah's faithful decision to invite *all* of God's people, divided into what functioned as different nations, to rehearse their *common* national identity through sincere participation in the Passover. Jesus knew this story backwards and forwards.

The fourth and fifth Passover stories are Josiah's (2 Kgs 23:21–25; 2 Chron 35:1–19). Josiah is the other good king in Chronicles. According to the Scriptures, good kings celebrate memorable Passovers, and the reader of Luke should be very unsurprised to see Jesus celebrating a memorable Passover.

The significance of Josiah's Passover was foreshadowed in 1 Kings 12–13. Rehoboam succeeds Solomon and asks the elders how to manage the labor of the people, to which the elders respond, in short, serve the people, and the people will serve you forever (12:1–7). Rehoboam rejects this advice; he rules harshly, like Pharaoh; and Israel responds by making Jeroboam their king (vv. 8–24). The fear of Jeroboam's heart is that Israel will return to Rehoboam, especially after going up to the house of Yahweh at Jerusalem to offer their sacrifices. Like Aaron, he fashions two golden calves, saying, "Behold your gods, O Israel, that brought you up from the land of Egypt." He goes on to build two new houses of worship, to form a new priesthood from *all* tribes, and, most pertinent to this study, to institute a new holiday: "And Jeroboam appointed a feast on the fifteenth day of the eighth month like the feast that was in Judah.... He went up to the altar that he had made in Bethel on the fifteenth day in the eighth month, in the month that he had devised from his own heart" (vv. 32–33). Jeroboam's whole festal institution, which parodies Yahweh's, is counted as a "sin to the house of Jeroboam," and the reason it will be "cut off" and "destroyed from the face of the earth" (13:34). Josiah is introduced in the middle of this story as the one through whom worship will be restored (13:1–3), signified in the breaking of Jeroboam's altar.

Jeroboam's contribution to the division of God's people was to invent a parodic festal institution which rivaled Yahweh's,

SUNDAY

explicitly designed to prevent Israel from returning to Jerusalem to keep their holidays.[4] That's what makes it so significant that Kings ends with Josiah's Passover story.

The version of the story in Kings is short, and it follows the basic pattern of Hezekiah's story. Josiah commands all the people to "'Keep the Passover to Yahweh *as it is written in this Book of the Covenant*.' For no such Passover had been kept since the days of the judges who judged Israel, or during all the days of the kings of Israel or of the kings of Judah" (2 Kgs 23:21–22).

But Josiah's Passover story ends oddly.

"After all of this," the Chronicler continues, Neco, the king of Egypt came up to fight at Carchemish and, for reasons undisclosed in the text, Josiah went out to meet him. Here is their puzzling exchange:

> [Neco] sent envoys to [Josiah], saying, "What have we to do with each other, king of Judah? I am not coming against *you* this day, but against the house with which I am at war. And God has commanded me to hurry. Cease opposing God, who is with me, lest he destroy you." Nevertheless, Josiah did *not* turn away from him, but disguised himself in order to fight with him. He did not listen to the words of Neco from the mouth of God, but came to fight in the plain of Megiddo. And the archers shot King Josiah. (2 Chron 35:21–23)

There are two riddles the text doesn't answer. First, even though thirteen years elapsed between the Feast and the Fight, the Chronicler tells this story *immediately* after that story. Why is that? The answer, I think, comes from the premise that liturgical history is concerned with the question of *how* God's people remember history, even the sequence of events, especially as those events relate to their liturgical calendar. Sure, Josiah dies thirteen years after his Passover, but the Chronicler wants God's people to

---

4. Jeroboam offers the Church a "figure" for bad holiday invention. We can read Edward Covey, for example, as walking in the spirit of Jeroboam: parodying a major religious feast, designed for unity and renewal, in order to keep people from returning to God.

4 PASSOVER PRESIDENT

remember the story of Josiah's death as happening "after *all this*" (v. 20), and who is to stop him? He is only doing what Numbers and Joshua have already done and what he had already done himself in chapters 31–32: immediately following up a Passover story with a story of some kind of Passover significance.

The second riddle is why Josiah "oppose[d] God" to take up a fight that didn't belong to him. Up to this point, the Chronicler has presented all of Josiah's decisions as righteous and, quite literally, "by the book." Until, that is, the Chronicler himself characterizes Neco's command as coming "from the mouth of God," which directly implies that Josiah ended his life with a fatal disobedience.

This is a common reading of Josiah: "Well, even the best kings aren't perfect." Josiah is a human person, and of course Josiah is not perfect. But is that the point of the story?

I don't think so. My interpretation, in short, is that in going out against Neco, Josiah did not "do bad," but rather did a good, Passover-themed thing. Here are three reasons.

One, Josiah knew that an Egyptian victory at Babylon would endanger Judah. Assyria was being besieged by Babylon, the newest empire on the block, and Egypt was coming to Assyria's aid. If Egypt could successfully defend Assyria against the attacks of Babylon, a "free" Assyria, who had defeated Israel two hundred years earlier, could hand Judah the same fate. To Josiah's mind, preventing Assyria's Egyptian ally meant safeguarding Judah from an old enemy.

Two, Josiah's reforms hadn't worked as well as Hezekiah's. Despite Josiah's earnest and thorough efforts, the testimonies of Jeremiah and Zephaniah strongly suggest that, in Judah, there continued to exist a widespread devotion to idols and that the people's one-hearted devotion to Yahweh around one altar didn't last very long. In the past, Yahweh has disciplined Israel by giving them into the hands of their enemies when they have been idolatrous, and Josiah knows this. If there was ever a time for Yahweh to allow Assyria to come in and knock Judah around, this would be the time. Josiah knows the international situation, he knows

SUNDAY

the sins of Judah, and he knows the hard discipline of Yahweh. Going out against Neco makes all the sense in the world.

Three, Neco is the king of—wait for it—*Egypt*. Even if the modern historian furrows his brow at the Chronicler telling two events that happened thirteen years apart as if they were a day apart, pay attention to what the Chronicler is doing. He moves quickly from the Passover—a commemoration of deliverance from Egypt—to the story of Israel's king doing battle against an Egyptian king. Josiah has just finished leading Israel in their celebration of "national deliverance" from Egypt. Here comes Egypt, who has allied themselves with Judah's greatest enemy, Assyria, claiming that the hand of God had brought them there. What is a king to do?

Josiah shows up. Neco is confused, and he asks essentially the same question that the demons will ask Jesus—"What have you to do with us, Jesus of Nazareth?" And Josiah teaches Neco what the Passover means to Israel: When you celebrate Yahweh's miraculous deliverance of His people, even the unfaithful ones, from the hand of their enemies, and then those same enemies claim to be doing God's work, you call "Blasphemy," strap on your sword, and do the right thing. Even if it means a young king following up his Passover celebration by dying to save God's people from the powers of darkness.[5]

Imagine where Jesus saw Himself in this story.

The sixth Passover story is Ezra's (6:19–22). And it makes sense that of all the books of the Bible, Ezra gets one of the Passover stories: The Passover celebrates the Exodus (Exod 12), and Ezra's Passover celebrates Israel's "Second Exodus" (Ezra 6). In Israel's early history, it takes them a long time—roughly 500 years—to complete their journey from captivity in Egypt to witnessing the

---

5. To be fair, this is a nontraditional interpretation of the story of Josiah's death. It is possible that Neco's warning *is* Yahweh's warning, and Josiah's cry of "Blasphemy!" is simply wrong. He dies not like the shepherd, David, throwing his life in front of a wolf to protect his sheep, but like the rash kings, Saul and Ahab, who enter a war that Yahweh has not given them. This story could be read instead as a *failed* Passover, such that readers should be concerned that Jesus' courageous Passover deliverance is a similar failure to listen to God's voice.

4 PASSOVER PRESIDENT

completion of Yahweh's house (1 Kgs 8). That is, their First Exodus isn't fulfilled for 500 years. Ezra tells the story of Israel's Second Exodus over the span of one generation and just six chapters of text. Despite its brevity, the Second Exodus story, from captivity to temple, follows the pattern of the first one. Rhys Laverty traces the pattern helpfully:

> As Ezra begins, God's people are in captivity in a foreign land—Persia, in this case, just as they had been in Egypt in Exodus. God took control of the heart of the king to deliver his people (Ez. 1:1; Ex. 4:14 etc.), so that they could leave the land, and build a house in which to worship him (Ez. 1:2–4; Ex. 3:18). As with Egypt, they left with great riches in their hands to get this done (Ez. 1:4–11; Ex. 12:36). This is all capped off with a Passover celebration (Ez. 6; Ex. 12).
>
> The grand story of the exodus is one of God giving *rest* to his people in the land—rest from their slavery, from their subsequent wilderness wandering, from the chaos of the days when the judges ruled. But mere *entry* into the land under Joshua doesn't achieve this rest; it's only accomplished by *settling* in the land when Solomon builds the temple. And so, when the temple is finished, Solomon declares: "Blessed be the LORD who has given *rest* to his people" (1 Ki. 8:56). The temple is the sign that the exodus is complete. Entering the land was like Israel coming home from a long journey, but building God's house was like putting their feet up.[6]

The observation that an exodus is not complete and that "rest" is not fully achieved until the temple is built makes sense of the Bible's previous Passover stories. Moses celebrates the Passover the day before Israel sets course for Canaan. Joshua celebrates the Passover at Canaan's door. Hezekiah celebrates the Passover once he restores temple worship, and so do Josiah and Ezra. This is one reason why the letter to the Hebrews says that Joshua did not give Israel rest and that "there remains a Sabbath

---

6. Rhys Laverty, "Ezra: The Aaronic Rest Giver," *Theopolis Institute Blog*, June 8, 2021, https://theopolisinstitute.com/ezra-the-aaronic-rest-giver/.

rest for the people of God" (Heb 4:9–10). Joshua only clears the ground; Solomon and Ezra finish building the temples.

The glaring difference between the Second Exodus and the First Exodus is the degree to which the respective kings supported Israel's celebration. Darius was very supportive; Pharaoh, of course, not so much.

In Egypt, Israel had supplied the lambs out of their own flocks. Pharaoh's generosity extends only so far as to permit them to do this: "Take your flocks and your herds, as you have said" (Exod 12:32).

Darius does so much more. But his story begins with Cyrus.

Cyrus had told Israel to "go up" to Jerusalem to build Yahweh a temple (Ezra 1). Opposition also rises, and several members of the "No Temple Party" seek political support from Artaxerxes, who disappoints Israel by giving them a stop-work order (Ezra 4–5). Enter Darius. He reinforces Cyrus's commission and adds his own measure of support. Before we read it, remember the Sabbatical manumission law from Deuteronomy 15. Pharaoh made Israel offer up their own lambs, and all the Sabbatical laws are written to make Israel more like Yahweh and less like Pharaoh:

> And when you let [your slave] go free from you, you shall not let him go empty-handed. *You shall furnish him liberally out of your flock*, out of your threshing floor, and out of your winepress. As Yahweh your God has blessed you, you shall give to him. You shall remember that you were a slave in the land of Egypt. (Deut 15:12–15)

Darius isn't a member of Israel, and he isn't bound by their laws. He may not even know them. Yahweh did not make a covenant with him, of which the Sabbath and the Sevenly Calendar had been given as a sign. And this makes it all the more wonderful that, in this instance, he rules according to the Spirit of the Sabbath:

> Moreover, I make a decree regarding what you shall do for these elders of the Jews for the rebuilding of this house of God. The cost is to be paid to these men in full and without delay from the royal revenue, the tribute of the province from Beyond the

River. And whatever is needed—bulls, rams, or sheep for burnt offerings to the God of heaven, wheat, salt, wine, or oil, as the priests at Jerusalem require—let that be given to them that day without fail, that they may offer pleasing sacrifices to the God of heaven. (Ezra 6:8–10)

Darius fulfills the Sabbath by restoring the edict of Cyrus, rebuking the people who opposed the construction of the temple, and releasing Israel—with provisions—to build Yahweh's house in a way that aimed at their rest.

Who eats the Passover lamb? More people than ever before: "the people of Israel who had returned from exile," plus "every one who had joined them and separated himself from the uncleanness of the peoples of the land to worship Yahweh, the God of Israel" (6:21). The priests and Levites preside over mixed tables, serving circumcised and uncircumcised alike, united in their decision to separate themselves, clean themselves, and cleave to Yahweh.

Passover Talk

Luke tells three Passover stories—Jesus Lost in the Temple (2); Jesus the Passover President (22); and Peter's Prison Passover (Acts 12). But he also presents Jesus talking about a big, future Passover: the Parousia Passover. Or, the moment when the Son of Man comes "at a time you do not expect." Here's what He says:

> Stay dressed for action (*humōn hai osphues periezōsmenai*) and keep your lamps burning, and be like men who are waiting for their master to come home from the wedding feast, so that they may open the door to him at once when he comes and knocks. Blessed are those servants whom the master finds awake when he comes. Truly, I say to you, he will dress himself for service and have them recline at table, and he will come and serve them. If he comes in the second watch, or in the third, and finds them awake, blessed are those servants! But know this, that if the master of the house had known at what hour *the thief* was coming, he would not have left his house to be broken into. You

also must be ready (*hetoimos*), for the Son of Man is coming at an hour you do not expect. (12:35–40)

Jesus takes His opening line from Exodus. He uses these words: *humōn hai osphues periezōsmenai*, woodenly translated, "your loins, let-them-be-girded." Yahweh had given Israel similar instructions for how to eat the Passover lamb: *hai osphues humōn periezōsmenai*, woodenly translated, "those loins of yours, let-them-be-girded (Exod 12:11 LXX).

The next hint Jesus gives that He will "come" like the Passover is that He expects His disciples to be ready at nighttime. Of course, Jesus' point isn't that He'll come between 11:00 pm and 3:00 am, Israel Standard Time (GMT +2:00). If He did that, it would be morning-time in Chicago, and all of us here in the Windy City would definitely be awake. No, Jesus does not mean some abstract notion of "nighttime," but the liturgical concept of the Passover night in particular. Remember the institution of the Passover vigil in Exodus 12:42: "It was a *night of watching* by Yahweh, to bring them out of the land of Egypt; so *this same night* is a *night of watching* kept to Yahweh by all the people of Israel throughout their generations." In the first month, on the fourteenth day of the month, at twilight. Waiting for the Son of Man to come will be just like waiting for Yahweh to come. Light your lamp, gird your loins, and be ready. The Passover remains a night of watching.

But the strangest thing Jesus says is that a thief is coming. For those of us who have the whole New Testament to look back on, this is not so strange. Paul says that "the day of the Lord will come like a thief in the night" (1 Thess 5:2), and Peter says the same thing (2 Pet 3:10). And then John sees Jesus Himself saying that He will "come like a thief" (Rev 3:3; 16:15).

But the first time He said it, Jesus may have caught His original audience off guard. Israel had been careful to clarify that Yahweh was *not* a thief. All the text of Exodus says is that "on that very day, Yahweh brought the people of Israel out of the land of Egypt by their hosts" (12:51). This leaves enough ambiguity that the *Mishnah Berakhot* dedicates half a chapter to distinguishing between the kinds of things Yahweh did during the Passover night and the kinds of things He waited to do until the morning. This clarification from the Chapters of Rabbi Eliezer explains why this distinction matters:

> The Holy One, blessed be He, said: If I bring forth the Israelites by night, they will say, He has done his deeds like a thief. Therefore, behold, I will bring them forth when the sun is in his zenith at midday. (48:20)

Earlier than that, the Book of Jasher (aka "The Book of the Upright") expressed the same concern in its imaginative retelling of the Exodus story:

> And the children of Israel delayed going forth at night, and when the Egyptians came to them to bring them out, they said to them, are we thieves, that we should go forth at night?[7]

Is Yahweh, the God of Israel's Exodus, a Passover thief? Prominent texts in Israel's tradition say, "No."

But the text of Exodus itself may suggest otherwise. Yahweh says that He has come down to "plunder" Israel from the power of the Egyptians (3:8). And when He tells Moses ahead of time that the women will ask their Egyptian neighbors for silver, gold, and clothing, He explains that this is the way they will "plunder the Egyptians" (3:22). When these instructions are fulfilled, the story concludes, "Thus they plundered the Egyptians" (12:36). Elsewhere in Luke, Jesus describes God as a strong man who encounters another "strong man, fully armed, [who] guards his own palace," and then "attacks him," "overcomes him," "takes away his armor," and "divides his spoil" (11:21–22).

Is Yahweh, the God of Israel's Exodus, a Passover thief? Rabbi Jesus disagrees with the tradition and says, "Yes."

Ten or so years later, He sends another angel to break the law by pinching Peter from prison (Acts 12). In Christ, Yahweh is

---

7. *Book of Jasher* 80:60.

SUNDAY

a thief, and the whole New Testament witness says He's coming back for more.

Jesus Keeps the Passover

Luke circles closer to the Passover moment in each paragraph. The first one begins, "Now the Feast of Unleavened Bread drew near, which is called the Passover" (22:1). Then Luke brings out the cast of bad guys. The chief priests and scribes are looking to get Him killed (v. 2), and Satan enters Judas (v. 3), who immediately begins colluding with them (vv. 4–6).

Next: "Then came the day of Unleavened Bread" (v. 7). Just as Yahweh instructed Israel to prepare the Passover in Exodus 12:1–13 and Numbers 9:9–14, and Hezekiah instructed all Israel and Judah in 2 Chronicles 30:1–9, and Josiah did in 35:1–6, Jesus instructs His disciples how to celebrate this particular Passover (vv. 7–13).

Finally: "When the hour came," the rite begins (v. 14). Jesus surrounds Himself with the twelve apostles, as Hezekiah called the twelve tribes. Standing in the shoes and fulfilling the role of every Passover president before Him, Jesus' opening words are straight from the heart: "I have earnestly desired to eat this Passover with you before I suffer" (v. 15). And His explanation follows from His piece about the Passover and the Parousia in Luke 12: "For I tell you I will not eat it until it is fulfilled in the kingdom of God" (v. 16).

Jesus won't eat the Passover with His disciples again until He comes back like a thief to grab the plunder of Jerusalem.[8] For

---

8. At this point, I would like to identify a theological divide which I intend to straddle for the sake of my readers. For those who take Jesus as foretelling the destruction of the temple in AD 70, these mentions of a "thief" and a "coming" are directly fulfilled within one generation. For those who take Jesus as foretelling the final destruction and rebuilding of the cosmos, these mentions of a "thief" and a "coming" will not be directly fulfilled until the end of history as we know it. I believe I can straddle these two interpretive schools because the *point* about Yahweh's Passover-patterned deliverances is that they are *all* patterned after the Passover and all recognized in the Church's Passover-like celebration of the Eucharist, in which we acknowledge all deliverances past and future. Therefore, in this chapter, I have written with an intentional ambiguity, assuming a mixed audience of adherents of post-

4 PASSOVER PRESIDENT

the sake of the time between now and then, He institutes a new liturgical commemoration that has come variously to be called the Holy Eucharist, the Lord's Supper, or Holy Communion. He takes bread and tells them that it is His body, broken and given for them. He takes the cup and tells them that it is the blood that solemnizes the new covenant.

The scene shifts immediately to a dispute over which is the greatest. Jesus gives His classic line about true leadership consisting of service, but the *way* He goes on to characterize such servanthood is often neglected. There's a drink they won't drink together until the kingdom of heaven comes, and there's a reason why they'll drink it together at all: "You are those who have *stayed with me in my trials*" (v. 28).

Their virtue consists in their "staying."

Therefore, He says, "I assign to you, as my Father assigned to me, a kingdom, that you may eat and drink at my table in my kingdom and sit on thrones judging the twelve tribes of Israel" (vv. 29–30).

And then Luke pours on the Passover irony.

Peter promises that he is "ready (*hetoimos*) to go with [Jesus] both to prison and to death" (v. 33). Luke has only used the word *hetoimos* two other times. Once, at 12:40, when Jesus says, "You also must be ready (*hetoimos*), for the Son of Man is coming at an hour you do not expect." And once more, in Luke 14, when the fabled host of the Great Banquet says "Everything is now ready (*hetoimos*)" (v. 17), after Jesus Himself says just a few lines up, "Blessed is everyone who will eat bread in the kingdom of God!" (v. 15). When Luke talks about being ready, he's only talking about one thing.

The one thing the disciples are being instructed to be ready for is the one thing Israel was instructed to be ready for in Egypt: the Thief coming in the night to deliver God's people and set out

---

millennial and amillennial doctrines and interpretations alike. For example, some may understand my phrase, "to grab the plunder of Jerusalem," as referring to AD 70, and others may understand "Jerusalem" more metaphorically, as referring to the world out of which Jesus calls His people.

a Great Banquet of bread and wine. There is a Great Banquet coming (Luke 12, 14), and the food is bread and wine (14, 22). That day is coming like a Thief (12); and it is the fulfillment of the Passover (12, 22). You'd best be "ready" (12, 14, 22).

Back to the story. Jesus goes out with His disciples to pray. And the disciples who had just been praised for "staying" with Jesus in His trials literally fall asleep (v. 45). Jesus wakes them up and points this out (v. 46). And literally "while he was still speaking," the Thief, Judas, comes in the night to take Jesus away.

Peter had said he was "ready to go with [Jesus] both to prison and to death." No, Peter was *not* ready to go with Jesus "on that night." Ten years later, however, Peter *will* go to prison. And, on the Passover, another delivering angel will appear, this one like the thief in Exodus, to wake him up and lead him out without asking permission. The apocryphal text, *The Martyrdom of Peter*, cited by Tertullian (2c.), Origen (3c.), and Jerome (5c.), says that Jesus appeared to Peter before Peter himself was crucified upside down. Jesus sent an angel to lead Peter out from prison, and the boundaries of Christian doctrine permit us to imagine that Jesus sent another angel to lead Peter through death into life incorruptible.

Luke communicates to his readers that the Church's new rite, which my tradition calls the Holy Eucharist, is continuous with Israel's Passover. What Israel experienced in Egypt (Exod 12), commemorated in order to abridge the story of unsettled-captivity to temple-rest (Num 10; Josh 5; 2 Kgs 23; 2 Chron 31, 35; Ezra 6; Luke 22), and kept as an expectation that Yahweh would deliver again, the Church inherits.

When the Church's celebrants lift up the bread and the cup, they stand in a long line of men who have been delivered out of captivity and look forward with expectation that Yahweh will send angels to move us along toward our final rest. We celebrate the Holy Eucharist to commemorate God's sending us out (Num 10), leading us in (Josh 5), finishing His temple (1 Kgs 8; Ezra 6), or restoring its service (2 Kgs 23; 2 Chron 31, 35). We remember, of course, that we are God's temple, "built on the foundation of the apostles and prophets, Christ Jesus himself being the cornerstone, in whom the whole structure, being joined together, grows into a holy temple in the Lord. In him you also are being built together into a dwelling place for God by the Spirit" (Eph 2:20–22).

The theological point of the Passover is the same as it always has been: Yahweh delivers His nation from captivity and leads them into rest. And that rest continues to include the Sabbatical ministry of release and the building of temples. The liturgical development is that Passover memory and expectation are now oriented toward Jesus' Parousia (Luke 12) and the Great Banquet (Luke 12, 14, 22).

Practically, we keep the Passover by making ourselves ready for Yahweh's deliverance. We ritually commemorate every one of Yahweh's great deeds of deliverance in the weekly rite of the Holy Eucharist. We fold into that celebration *all* of His acts of deliverance, both large and small. And all of our thanksgiving for Yahweh's deeds of deliverance aims at making us ready for every new coming of the angelic Thief, as we remain ready for His Parousia.

5 LUKE'S FIRST DAY

"And the day after Passover, on that very day, they ate of the produce of the land."
Joshua 5:11

"Christ has been raised from the dead, the firstfruits of those who have fallen asleep."
1 Corinthians 15:20

Luke tells the story of Jesus' resurrection, which he frames with the same time marker as the resurrection stories in the other three Gospels. Here is Luke's: "*On the first day of the week*, at early dawn…" (24:1). Now here are the other three:

> "Now after the Sabbath, toward the dawn of *the first day of the week* …" (Matt 28:1)
>
> "Very early *on the first day of the week*, when the sun had risen …" (Mark 16:2)
>
> "Now *on the first day of the week* … early, while it was still dark …" (John 20:1)

The phrase "the first day of the week" appears two more times in the New Testament: once in a set of liturgical instructions given by Paul (1 Cor 16:1–4) and again at the beginning of another one of Luke's stories (Acts 20:7–12).

What is the Old Testament significance of this time marker?

On the first day of the *first* week, Yahweh said "Let there be light" (Gen 1:3–5). Paul notices this and exclaims that, in Christ, that same God who said "Let there be light" has shone in our hearts, making us new creations (2 Cor 4:6).

Nice.

But the premise and the fundamental insight of this chapter is that this particular "first day of the week" happens to be the first day of the week that directly follows the Passover (Luke 22:1; cf. Lev 23:4–8). Remember the Calendar. The Sunday (first day after the Sabbath) after the Passover is the Feast of Firstfruits (Lev 23:9–14).

God raised Jesus on the Feast of Firstfruits.[1]

That's the punchline.

When Yahweh instituted the Feast of Firstfruits and commanded Israel to commemorate it liturgically each year, He intended that this annual commemoration would prepare Israel to commemorate His new work of raising Jesus from the dead. Paul got *this* connection, too, and he tells us, in a passage chock full of agrarian metaphors, that "Christ has been raised from the dead, the *firstfruits* of those who had fallen asleep" (1 Cor 15:20).

Again, nice.

Paul caught this so quickly because Israel already knew that Firstfruits was a resurrection feast. This chapter will begin with an explanation of the Feast of Firstfruits as it is described

---

1. There is a minor controversy, but Thiessen demonstrates that "the majority of Rabbinic Jews regarded השבת in Lev 23:11 as referring to the day following the Passover" in Jacob Thiessen, "Firstfruits and the Day of Christ's Resurrection: An Examination of the Relationship between the 'Third Day' in 1 Cor 15:4 and the 'Firstfruit' in 1 Cor 15:20," *Neotestamentica 46*, no. 2 (2012): 382–87. See also Daniel K. Bediako, "The Sheaf Offering and Resurrection Sunday," *Asia-Africa Journal of Mission and Ministry 16* (August 2017): 122–27; Harold Louis Ginsberg, "The Grain Harvest Laws of Leviticus 23:9–22 and Numbers 28:26–31," *Proceedings of the American Academy for Jewish Research 46*, 47 (1979): 141–53; Jacob Milgrom, *Leviticus 23–27*, Anchor Bible (New Haven: Yale, 2001).

in Leviticus 23:9–14 and Israel's liturgical manuals. Then, it will discuss the New Testament's use of the term "firstfruits" and the two other places in the New Testament which discuss "the first day of the week."

In the first four chapters, I have demonstrated that the Scriptures disclose Yahweh's holidays in at least a threefold way. First, they tell their origin stories, that is, Yahweh's particular acts of deliverance that each holiday uniquely commemorates. Second, they provide legislation explaining how to keep each particular holiday, both liturgically and ethically. Third, they tell the stories of how the holidays are kept throughout history, which is how they accumulate meaning.

In this chapter, I am arguing that the New Testament does a similar thing. It tells the origin story of the new Christian holiday, called "the first day of the week" in all four Gospels (Matt 28; Mark 16; Luke 24; John 20–21), when Yahweh delivers Jesus from death. Paul provides liturgical and ethical instructions for making offerings (1 Cor 16:1–4). And Luke tells the first big "first day" story in Church history (Acts 20:7–12).

The Feast of Firstfruits

Following its descriptions of the Sabbath (Lev 23:3) and the Passover (vv. 4–8), the Calendar describes Israel's two harvest festivals: vv. 9–14 describe the ritual offering of barley, called "Firstfruits" (vv. 9–14), which takes place on the first day after the Sabbath after Passover (v. 11); and vv. 15–22 describe the first offering of wheat, called the "Feast of Weeks," or "Pentecost," seven weeks after the day of the initial barley offering (vv. 15–16).

In the Old Testament, the term "firstfruits" refers sometimes to this feast and the offering which corresponds to it, and sometimes to the Feast of Weeks and its offering (e.g. Lev 23:17–20; 2 Kgs 4:42). It is also used both ways in Israel's liturgical manuals, which describe a tight relationship between what Leviticus describes as two distinct feasts. See, for example, *Jubilees* 6:20–21:

And do thou command the children of Israel to observe this festival in all their generations for a commandment unto them: one day in the year in this month they shall celebrate the festival. For it is the feast of weeks and the feast of firstfruits: this feast is twofold and of a double nature; according to what is written and engraven concerning it, celebrate it.

Despite the documentary evidence of these two feasts being combined—at some times, in some ways—there is also plenty of commentary treating the two feasts as distinct liturgical institutions with their own internal logic. This chapter will stick to the *first* Firstfruits.

The "first" in "firstfruits" does not refer to the fruits that ripen the fastest, nor does it refer to the highest quality fruits. It simply refers, in the sequential sense, to the first of the fruits that are harvested. In the popular words of Rabbi Saadia ben Joseph, Israel offered the first fruits of their harvest to Yahweh because "it is not good manners to eat of the new (crop) until you bring a gift before the Holy One, Blessed be He."[2]

The "fruits" in "firstfruits" refers to barley, at least according to Leviticus. In Israel's liturgical manuals, however, there are seven acceptable "fruits": wheat, barley, grapes, figs, pomegranates, olive oil, and date honey (*m. bik.* 1:10).[3]

According to Leviticus 23:9–14, the Firstfruits rite consists of two parts. First, the priest waves the sheaf, and the offerer offers a lamb as an ascension offering (v. 12). By offering an ascension offering, the priest sets the tone for the barley offerings that follow, making the whole ritual a properly sacrificial rite. Then the people, or at least each of the land-owning members of the community, are to present barley offerings from the harvests of each of their own households.

When these land-owning community members brought barley, they did not bring it in the form of *sheaves*, right from farm to

---

2. Cited in Milgrom, *Leviticus 23–27*, 1984.

3. Other biblical texts (e.g. 2 Kgs 4:42–44; Neh 10:34–39) provide other lists. However, since these texts do not function as comprehensive liturgical manuals, the two texts I've cited above seem more helpful.

table. They brought barley-based cereal offerings. Someone had to know how to bake. They were expected to apply "work" to the barley: crushing it and roasting it in the home and then forming it into cakes. Farm to kitchen to table.

Mm. Artisanal barley.

This in-home ritual of food preparation would make it match the "freewill" offerings described earlier in Leviticus (7:11–18; 22:18–23). Barley offerings, and all fruit offerings, are not raw, but cooked.

The purpose of the ritual offering of barley cakes by land-owning Israelites was to commemorate Yahweh's having settled them into the new land. You can see this most clearly in Leviticus 23:10, where Yahweh divides their early history into two periods: There is the time *before* Israel reaps her first harvest in the new land, and there is the time *after* Israel reaps her first harvest in the new land. These are two different times. He instructs Israel *not* to observe Firstfruits until "you come into the land that I give you and reap its harvest."

Some nervous commentators, not taking this clause very seriously, have speculated that Israel must have begun observing Firstfruits while they were still wandering with Moses in the wilderness, offering "seeds." But offering seeds would have missed the point entirely. And it distracts from the significance of Joshua's Passover story (Josh 5:10–12), which ends with Israel eating "the fruit of the land of Canaan" the very next day. *That* was the first Firstfruits.

Yahweh's rule against celebrating too soon matters because it reminds us that Firstfruits is not an abstract principle, like, "We give all of our 'firsts' to God." (Some have speculated that Yahweh does not accept Cain's offering of the "fruit of the ground" because he offered it before Abel offered meat and fat from his flock. First come meat offerings; then come fruit offerings. Whether or not they're onto something, it's at least a helpful illustration).

Yahweh's acts in history matter. Like the Sabbath, the Passover, and all of Israel's other holidays, Firstfruits is a liturgical commemoration of Yahweh's deliverance of Israel. The Passover commemorates Yahweh's deliverance from out of Egypt; Firstfruits commemorates Yahweh's deliverance *into* Canaan. Moses celebrates the Passover, but he knows better than to celebrate a harvest that Yahweh hasn't given him yet. Joshua celebrates both the Passover and Firstfruits because he is commemorating a significant shift in Israel's history. Yahweh and His Israel have a real history, and their holidays do more than acknowledge and reinforce universal moral principles.

Scripture tells a handful of stories of people celebrating the Passover, but it tells no stories of people celebrating Firstfruits. After Deuteronomy, the Old Testament won't explicitly refer to the feast of Firstfruits again.[4] Most of what we know about how and when Firstfruits is celebrated comes from other sources, like the *Mishnah Bikkurim* (*m. bik.*), the *Book of Jubilees* (*Jub.*), and Moses Maimonides's *Bikkurim* (*bik.*). Among these, the *Mishnah Bikkurim* is an explanation of Firstfruits traditions in the Talmud, which contains Israel's most authoritative liturgical teachings besides the Scriptures themselves. By raising Jesus on the Feast of Firstfruits, Yahweh directly fulfills the Scriptures and critically fulfills Israel's liturgical tradition that fleshes out the Scriptures.[5]

Commenting on the set of ritual instructions at Deuteronomy

---

4. Although it will mention the offering itself in 2 Kings 4:42; 2 Chron 31:5; Neh 10:35; 12:44; 13:1.

5. It is a theme of both the Old Testament and the New Testament that Israel keeps the Sabbath badly. It is a theme of the *Gospels* that there is confusion about the meaning of the Passover. We don't read anything about Firstfruits being a corrupt institution in need of correction, and I think we can largely understand it as a "forgotten" institution in need of exposition. This also frames the ways in which we handle the relevant extrabiblical literature. In discussions of the Sabbath, we do best to follow Jesus back to the sources and then draw from extrabiblical sources, like 11QMelchizedek, in so far as they faithfully express or develop the relevant biblical literature. In discussions of the Passover, we might have found *more* useful extrabiblical material, like important speeches and observance narratives. In this discussion of Firstfruits, the extrabiblical material largely serves to *clarify* and *flesh out* the little biblical material we have. This chapter will attend closely to the biblical material, and it will also attend to the helpful material we have in these other sources. I hope the reader agrees that the two don't appear to come into very significant conflict and that Jesus' (direct) fulfillment of the Scriptures is also an (indirect) fulfillment of these liturgical traditions as they faithfully express what Yahweh instituted in Scripture.

26:1–11, these other sources describe the Firstfruits rite as consisting of seven steps.

First, the *bikkurim* (which are the fruits themselves) must be brought to Jerusalem and, when the temple is standing, the *bikkurim* must be brought to Jerusalem's temple. Jews in the Diaspora loved the Feast of Firstfruits because it was the only time in the liturgical calendar when they were permitted to send personal offerings along to Jerusalem even when they could not attend themselves. Diaspora Jews who "mailed in" their offerings dried their grapes and figs.

But those who could get themselves to Jerusalem were required to bring their *bikkurim* into the temple itself in a corporate procession, and they brought them fresh. All the offerers from the various cities would gather together the night before the Firstfruits procession and camp outside in order to make sure they remained ceremonially pure. At the crack of dawn, one of the city's officers would ritually proclaim the words from Jeremiah, "Let us arise and go up to Zion, into the house of the Lord our God" (31:5). They would be greeted at the Temple by a cohort of officers and artisans who would respond with the ritual words, "Our brothers, men of such and such a place, we welcome you in peace" (*m. bik.* 3:3).

Once the procession arrived at the temple mount to the sound of flutes, the Levite singers would intone Psalm 30, the song which would come to characterize the Firstfruits liturgy (*m. bik.* 3:4):

> I will extol you, O Yahweh, for you have drawn me up
>   and have not let my foes rejoice over me.
> O Yahweh my God, I cried to you for help,
>   and you have healed me.
> O Yahweh, you have brought up my soul from Sheol;
>   you restored me to life from among those who go down to the pit. (Psalm 30:1–3)

The song choice makes sense. "You have brought up my soul from Sheol" corresponds to Yahweh's having brought up Israel from Egypt and from the wilderness. But these words are particularly interesting because of the resurrection traditions surrounding them.

The Levites would have sung Psalm 30 in its entirety. And even according to Israel's own tradition of interpreting Psalm 30, it's not crazy to think "resurrection." For one, there are the words right on the surface. It's about Yahweh bringing the soul up from Sheol and restoring him to life. If you're not thinking "resurrection," you're already starting on the wrong foot.

In a section that explains Leviticus 23:10, a midrash on Leviticus called the *Vayikra Rabbah* recounts the tradition that Mordecai sang Psalm 30 to commemorate his exaltation on the day of Israel's deliverance. The *Vayikra Rabbah* points out that Mordecai finds favor with the king specifically on "the third day." It points out that Jonah, too, was in the belly of a fish for three days (Jonah 1:17) and that Joseph imprisoned his brothers for three days (Gen 42:17).

"Three days" became Israel's shorthand for "about how long Yahweh leaves His faithful ones buried." Hosea makes use of this three-days tradition in one place, where he confidently says, "On the third day [Yahweh] will raise us up" (6:2). Why? Yahweh raises His faithful ones on the third day.

My point here is admittedly a foggy one. On the Feast of Firstfruits, Israel sang Psalm 30. Psalm 30 is about Yahweh raising His faithful ones up from Sheol. And they understood that Yahweh has a pattern of raising His faithful ones up from Sheol on "the third day." In short, Israel spent the Feast of Firstfruits singing a psalm which was associated with a third-day resurrection. When Paul says that Jesus rose on the third day, "according to the Scriptures" (1 Cor 15:4), scholars think he had this traditional "third day" pattern in mind.[6] This string of associations proves nothing definitively; let the reader furrow his brow. Back to the ritual.

Once the offerings were brought into the temple, they would be placed on the ground or handed to a priest. Once the offerer had brought it that far, he would have fulfilled his responsibility.

---

6. See, for example, David Instone-Brewer, *Traditions of the Rabbis from the Era of the New Testament 1: Prayer and Agriculture* (Grand Rapids: Eerdmans, 2004), 410.

SUNDAY

Why? *M. bik.* 1:9 points out that Exodus 23:19 requires only that "the first of the firstfruits of your land *you shall bring into the house of the Lord your God.*"

Second, the *bikkurim* would be brought in a container of some kind, often a basket. That way the priest could take it himself and do what priests are hired to do.

Third, the offerer must recite "the Declaration," which comes from Deuteronomy 26:5–10. Yahweh instructs the offerer of *bikkurim* to say the ritual words as they bring their *bikkurim*:

> A wandering Aramean was my father. And he went down into Egypt and sojourned there, few in number, and there he became a nation, great, mighty, and populous. And the Egyptians treated us harshly and humiliated us and laid on us hard labor. Then we cried to Yahweh, the God of our fathers, and Yahweh heard our voice and saw our affliction, our toil, and our oppression. And Yahweh brought us out of Egypt with a mighty hand and an outstretched arm, with great deeds of terror, with signs and wonders. And he brought us into this place and *gave us this land*, a land flowing with milk and honey. And behold, now I bring the first of the fruit of *the ground, which you, O Yahweh, have given me.*

The offerer of *bikkurim* is instructed to identify himself with the people who experienced the Exodus. (Remember Israel's liturgical principle: "In every generation one must see himself as if he has come out of Egypt.") What makes this Declaration a distinctly "Firstfruits" declaration is the final two sentences about Yahweh's having given the offerer his land.

Who was allowed to say these words? The *Mishnah* explains in detail who can and who cannot declare the collective words "the God of *our* fathers" and "gave *us* this land." These were boundary markers for who counted as a true Israelite (*m. bik.* 1:4–11). It also uses this text to reemphasize and explain why only landowners offer Firstfruits, and not sharecroppers, renters, or squatters. The Scripture says that the *bikkurim* are the firstfruits of *your* land, not someone else's (*m. bik.* 1:2; cf. Exod 23:19).

And the Declaration says in the first person singular that the *bikkurim* had come from the ground "which you, O Yahweh, have given *me*" (Deut 26:10). Remember that the Sabbath command was given to a singular head of household, "you," who was responsible both for his own rest as well as for the rest of his whole household? These details matter when we think about how Jesus fulfills these holidays and how the Church receives them.

The *Mishnah* also envisions offerers who have memorized these words reciting them first, and then those who do not have them memorized, but need some help, repeating them after the priests (*m. bik.* 3:7).

Fourth, the *bikkurim* must be "waved" by the priest. Per Leviticus, "one of the priests shall wave it" (23:11). Moses Maimonides specifies that they are to be waved "up and down and to all four directions" (*Bik.* 3:12). If you've ever attended a ritually-sophisticated Anglican mass, or a Roman Catholic one, you're likely to have seen the celebrating priest move the ritual bread up and down and in all four directions. And now you know where they get it from.

Fifth, as I pointed out above, the *bikkurim* must be accompanied by a peace offering.

Sixth, since peace offerings are meant to be eaten, the point is that both the offerer and the priest would eat the peace offering together. Meat turns an offering into a feast. The one extra rule is that, because Deuteronomy 26:11 states that "you shall rejoice in all the good," the tradition understands that eating the peace offering while in a state of "acute mourning" would make one ritually impure (*bik.* 3:5–6).

Seventh, because the Passover instructions at Deuteronomy 16:7 say, "And you shall turn back in the morning and return to your tent," and because the tradition takes this as a general festal principle, the offeror is obligated to stay the night in Jerusalem (*bik.* 3:14). I'm persuaded that whoever wrote this requirement must have had a nephew working in Jerusalem's hotel industry. Special interests. *Tsk, tsk.* Or maybe it was to prevent driving home under the influence. There's a dissertation topic for someone in there.

Outside this sevenfold ritual framework, Firstfruits appears to have been a relatively unregulated feast. Neither Scripture nor tradition told people how much fruit to bring. The various processions were characterized by local customs. There were rules requiring joyful participation, but none legislating exactly how to make joy. We all know people who are good at planning parties, running games, and otherwise facilitating fun. There's no reason to believe Firstfruits wasn't their time to shine.

Leviticus fixes Firstfruits on the day after the Sabbath after the Passover, seven sevens of days before Pentecost, a word which means "fifty" (Lev 23:15–16; *Jub.* 6:21; 16:13; 22:1). But so long as the *bikkurim* was offered sometime before the Feast of Tabernacles, it would have been accepted. That's a significant contrast to the Sabbath, which had to be celebrated on the seventh day, and the Passover, which the Scriptures take pains to say was celebrated in the first month, on the fourteenth day, at twilight.

Firstfruits in the New Testament

The New Testament uses the same word, "firstfruits" (*aparchē*), eight times, and it consistently uses the word to mean the same thing. Paul uses it twice to explain the logical relationship between Christ's resurrection and our own in 1 Corinthians 15. In vv. 12–19 of that chapter, Paul considers his opponents' premise that "there is no resurrection of the dead" (v. 12). If Paul grants this premise, the first consequence is that we cannot say that Christ has been "raised" (v. 15), and the second is that "those also who have fallen asleep in Christ" are also goners (v. 18). If there really is no resurrection of the dead, then those of us who proclaim that God raised Jesus and believe that He will raise us with Him "are of all people most to be pitied" (v. 19). Paul retorts,

> But in fact Christ has been raised from the dead, the firstfruits (*aparchē*) of those who have fallen asleep. For as by a man came death, by a man has come also the resurrection of the dead. For

5 LUKE'S FIRST DAY

as in Adam all die, so also in Christ shall all be made alive. But each in his own order: Christ the firstfruits (*aparchē*), then at his coming those who belong to Christ. (vv. 20–23)

Paul assures the Church of their resurrection by identifying them liturgically as the rest of the barley harvest.
Here's how the metaphor plays out.
The world is the Lord's, and so is its fullness. He's a vinedresser. At the appointed time, at the Harvest of Humanity, Christ is the first to be harvested, and so He is called the firstfruits. Picked, prepared, put in a basket, brought up to the temple to the tune of Psalm 30 played on flutes, waved, and eaten by priest and people. He is the cluster of grapes who identifies the cup of wine as the blood of His new covenant; the sheaf of barley pressed into cakes who Himself lifts up bread and says, "This is my body"; the cluster of olives who is crushed in an olive grove called Gethsemane. Growing in other rows alongside Him, or as members grafted into the same vine, are all those who have fallen asleep in Him. Jesus is the first *bikkurim* offering who sacralizes the remainder of the harvest. Ha. The *bikkurim* ritual was a resurrection and ascension liturgy all along. If Jesus is plucked and taken into God's house, so will we be.

The world is the Lord's, but it is still divided into nations and regions and cities. Four times, the New Testament uses the term *aparchē* to refer to the first "crop" of converts from one of those nations, regions, or cities. In 1 Corinthians 15:20 and 23, Jesus is the firstfruits "of those who have fallen asleep." In 16:15–18, *aparchē* refers to a whole household:

> You know that the household of Stephanas were the first converts (*aparchē*) in Achaia, and that they have devoted themselves to the service of the saints—be subject to these, and to every fellow worker and laborer. I rejoice at the coming of Stephanas and Fortunatus and Achaicus, because they have made up for your absence, for they refreshed my spirit as well as yours. Give recognition to such people.

SUNDAY

Ignoring the fact that the ESV obscures Paul's third use of *aparchē* by translating it "converts," thereby robbing Stephanas and his household of an incredibly flattering comparison to Jesus Christ, notice the relationship of Stephanas to his region and to Paul. Christ is the firstfruits of those who have fallen asleep. And now these living persons, Stephanas's household, are the firstfruits of the particular "field" called Achaia: harvested, prepared, put in a basket, carried into the household of God, and "refreshing" to priestly figures like Paul who make living *bikkurim* out of people.

Paul uses *aparchē* the same way in Romans: "Greet my beloved Epaenetus, who was the first convert (*aparchē*) to Christ in Asia" (16:5). It is well known that Paul lists twenty-six friends by name in this chapter and that he honors each of them differently. Note now that, of the twenty-six friends, Epaenetus is the only one who is identified by the place where he lives *and* that he is the only one honored as *aparchē*. Go back and look. This is not a coincidence. *Aparchē* does not mean, flatly, "convert." *Aparchē* is an Old Testament liturgical concept and a New Testament metaphor that describes the first fruits to be harvested among a particular household or region and a celebration of the fact that Yahweh has given the land to His people. That Epaenetus was harvested from Asia bodes well for Asia. More will follow.

James uses *aparchē* nearly the same way as Paul. Writing to Jewish believers who have been flung out broadly in the Diaspora (1:1) and reminded that their lives are like the flowers of the field (1:9–11), he tells them that, wherever they have found themselves, they are "a kind of firstfruits (*aparchē*) of his creatures" (1:18). Even though their experience feels like exile, and in some literal sense *is* an exile, in the new covenant, Yahweh has given all of the land to Jesus, and the dignity of the fading flower is that it may yet be offered as firstfruits. James dignifies these exiled men and women the same way Paul honors Stephanas of Achaia and Epaenetus of Asia.

John uses *aparchē* along the same lines. As in 1 Corinthians 15:20 and 23, the scope is not one particular region, but the whole earth. Anyone who knows John knows that John thinks big thoughts. The 144,000 martyrs whom John sees in his vision are those who "had been redeemed from the earth." Like good *bikkurim*, they are undefiled, and they follow the Lamb wherever He goes: "They have been redeemed from mankind as firstfruits (*aparchē*) for God and the Lamb, and in their mouth no lie was found, for they are blameless" (14:3–4).

Firstfruits and the First Day

The New Testament uses the phrase "on the first day" two more times. The first one is at 1 Corinthians 16:2, immediately after the passage in which Paul identifies Jesus as "the firstfruits of those who have fallen asleep." "The first day" is shorthand for "Firstfruits," so we shouldn't be surprised that the one time that Paul identifies Jesus as "firstfruits" is followed by the one time he mentions "the first day." Here's the text:

> Now concerning the collection for the saints: as I directed the churches of Galatia, so you also are to do. *On the first day of every week*, each of you is to put something aside and store it up, as he may prosper, so that there will be no collecting when I come. And when I arrive, I will send those whom you accredit by letter to carry your gift to Jerusalem. If it seems advisable that I should go also, they will accompany me. (16:1–4)

Yes, Paul instructs the Corinthians to make offerings "on the first day" of the week. This fact alone doesn't *prove* that Paul views this offering as an application of the *bikkurim* offering. But look a little closer and notice some of the resonances. Here are seven:

One, *as I directed the churches of Galatia, you also are to do*. Why does Paul preface his instructions by telling them that he's already given these instructions to the churches of Galatia? Paul may be motivated by efficiency, really wanting to make sure that "the saints" get this collection before they starve. Maybe Paul is trying to brand himself as a philanthropy coach. More than likely, though, Paul is pointing out that he is giving "common instructions" about how to make offerings to the whole Israel of God. Where in the Bible have we seen someone instruct all of God's

SUNDAY

people to make their offerings with certain guidelines? How about the five offerings in Leviticus 1–7? How about the *Mishnah Bikkurim*? This short paragraph from 1 Corinthians 16 is Paul's New Testament version of the Old Testament's "ceremonial law."

When Paul says he "directed" the churches of Galatia, he uses the word *diatassō*, which has military connotations. When Paul directed these churches, he assembled them like a battalion of offerers. (Is this part of what it means to be a kingdom of priests?)

But as true as this is, we don't even need to dwell on the military connotations because only a moment ago, Paul has just used the word *tagma*, which is the root of *diatassō*, to talk about firstfruits and the resurrection: "But each in his own order (*tagma*): Christ the *aparchē*, then at his coming those who belong to Christ" (15:23). If the translators wanted to press the lexical connection between the two words, they might have said, "But each in his own place in the liturgical procession," in the first passage, and "As I organized the liturgical procession in the churches of Galatia" in the second.

On "the first day of the week," the Church in multiple places makes her offerings in an orderly way that corresponds to the order of Christ's resurrection and of the liturgical concept of firstfruits.

Two, *on the first day of every week*. The offering that corresponds to the *bikkurim* offering is no longer an annual offering but a weekly one. This follows the trends we've already seen in the Sabbath and the Passover. Israel celebrated the Sabbath every week, but Jesus proclaimed the acceptable *year* of the Lord and the *age* of the Sabbath. Every day is a day for rebuking the powers, releasing those under your care, and participating in Christ's rest. The annual Passover commemoration will eventually give way to Easter, but not before it is established as a weekly commemoration of Christ's death and resurrection. So, too, with Firstfruits. We now make our offerings on the first day of *every* week.

This, by way of reminder, is the argument both of this chapter and of this book. Luke takes Israel's weekly commemoration and two of her annual commemorations, mixes them together, and shows his readers what the new Christian holiday, "Sunday," means. Sunday is a combination of the Passover and Firstfruits with the Sabbath.

Three, *each one of you ... as he may prosper*. The responsibility for making the firstfruits offering had fallen to landowning heads of household only. That is, those who were allowed to say the ritual words in Deuteronomy 26, Yahweh "gave *us this* land." In these instructions, Paul broadens both the responsibility and the opportunity of making "first day" offerings to include everyone: "each of you," he says.

Paul does love his agrarian metaphors, but he also knows they're metaphors. He's not collecting fruit; he's collecting money. And lots of people make money, not just the dad who runs the family farm. But in the new covenant, Yahweh has given the whole earth to Jesus, and Jesus has accepted His appointment as head of the whole household. Remember that He heals a woman in the synagogue (Luke 13:10–17) because He identifies her as His daughter, and the Sabbath Command requires that a head of household provide rest for his daughters (Exod 20:8–11). Luke shows us in this story, implicitly, that Jesus is the head of every household.

Paul is more explicit. "The head of every man is Christ," Paul says earlier in Corinthians (11:3). As a result, "All things are yours" (3:21).

This is why "each of you" is permitted to make an offering: In the new covenant, the land has been divided up differently. Yahweh has given Jesus all the land, and He has, in turn, given it to His people. The Corinthians' offerings, the Galatians' offerings, and now our offerings commemorate that Yahweh has given this land to Jesus. The fruits of the whole earth are His, and of His own have we given Him. This is not a timeless moral principle, but a liturgical rite that commemorates Yahweh's having given all the land to Jesus and having made Him head of every man. Paul organizes us and gives us a place in the processional line.

Neither the Scripture nor the tradition requires a precise amount of *bikkurim*, and neither does Paul. Israelites came into their land at different times, and some never really settled. So it is with God's people today. You've got families with a two-flat and a vacation home in Wisconsin; and you've got other families who are renting basement apartments. You need not be a landowner to make a "first day" offering, but each person is invited to make his offering "as he may prosper."

Four, *put something aside and store it up*. Offerers of the *bikkurim* did not offer sheaves of barley, but they applied work, turning them into barley cakes. Those who didn't travel to Jerusalem dried their grapes and their figs. Those who harvested dates turned them into honey. That households would ritually prepare their own *bikkurim* offerings had an effect of sanctifying the menial labors of meal prep. Money is not nearly as romantic or as holy as food, but there is something to the liturgical (weekly) and ritual (for an offering) action of putting it aside and storing it up.

Every church bookkeeper wants parishioners to automate their tithes through PayPal so that they don't accidentally forget to give when they're on vacation. They will point out that Paul didn't have PayPal and that he certainly would have made use of that tool had he been born way later. (Is there room here for a PayPaul joke? That's not a dissertation topic. That's a potential tech start-up!)

But every typological liturgist wants his people to be formed by the ritual, embodied act of "putting aside" and "storing up" and then giving "as he may prosper." That helps him participate in Christ's fulfillment of the Feast of Firstfruits, and it teaches him how to weekly commemorate that God has made Christ the head of every man and given all things to us. And these liturgists think that Paul agrees with *them*. Good luck.

Five, *so that there will be no collecting when I come*. This may be an appeal to efficiency, or to the Passover value of being ready. But it also has a formative aspect: Making this offering is a disciplined response to the liturgical calendar, not a spontaneous response to a Christian leader. Again, Paul is organizing the Church into a liturgical procession of offerers that follows the pattern of the resurrection of Jesus the Firstfruits. This is not accomplished by telling a sob story while the worship leader slowly fades in some background piano music on the synth, layered over a heart-stirring pad of strings. It's accomplished by pointing people to a meaningful liturgical calendar and telling them how to keep it.

In the United States, each president presents and defends a federal budget and a tax plan that makes it feasible. In their campaign work, they pitch their tax plans as tough on the rich, encouraging small business, expanding the middle class, or relieving the poor. These tax plans, with their brackets and their exemptions, are not received traditions, but new documents rewritten each year by presidents and their advisors.

Remember that this was the point of the Manumission Law, Sabbath Year, and Year of Jubilee: Forgiveness, pardon, and manumission were regulated by the Sevenly Calendar and not left to political and economic expediency or the whims of rulers. People will be restored to their land when the Calendar says—not when the bank says, not right after the campaign promise is made, and not when the landlord decides. In a truly Sabbatical world, presidents would be beholden to rhythms of seven and forty-nine years. The "loan forgiveness" they might administer would not be part of their platform, but participation in an enduring social institution, expected at a fixed time. Paul puts aside his own authority and influence and asks the churches simply to keep the New Testament iteration of Yahweh's Sevenly Calendar.

Six, *to carry your gift to Jerusalem*. This matches the pattern of *bikkurim*. Those who live far from Jerusalem, like the Corinthians, are not required to travel to Jerusalem every Sunday, but may send proxies. But all the gifts are still supposed to go to Jerusalem, and now, the New Jerusalem.

Seven, *if it seems advisable that I should go also, they will accompany me*. Paul does not say that he needs to facilitate the giving, but that he is willing to help facilitate them. I think this is because Paul consistently identifies Christian generosity as a ritual offering. My inclination to read Paul's instructions to the Corinthians as prioritizing Christian formation over economic efficiency came out of this passage from his letter to the Philippians.

SUNDAY

Notice how Paul identifies this offering formationally and liturgically:

> Not that I seek the gift, but I seek the fruit that increases to your credit. I have received full payment, and more. I am well supplied, having received from Epaphroditus the gifts you sent, a fragrant offering, a sacrifice acceptable and pleasing to God. (4:17–18)

It's right there. First, he says that he seeks the profit of the giver more than the profit of the recipient. That's a focus on formation. Second, he literally calls their gift "a fragrant offering, a sacrifice acceptable and pleasing to God." That's straight out of Leviticus (e.g., 1:9). And it's another prooftext for our axiom that Christian formation is liturgical and that we ought to imagine and describe the Church's activities using liturgical and ritual categories. Just like Paul.

Paul's instructions to the Corinthians are a New Testament *torah*. Just as the Old Testament combines the story of the Passover with liturgical instructions for how to keep it (e.g., Exod 12; Lev 23:4–8), the New Testament combines the story of "the first day of the week" (Matt 28; Mark 16; Luke 24; John 20) with liturgical instructions for how to keep it (1 Cor 16:1–4). In this case, Paul would have the Church commemorate the resurrection of Jesus, the Firstfruits, by joining Jesus' liturgical procession and offering the "fruits" of their own labor since Yahweh has given the world to Jesus, since Christ is now head of every man, and since that means that all things are ours.

Luke's "First Day" Resurrection Story

Jesus rises "on the first day of the week," and He is not the only one. The only other "first day of the week" story in the New Testament is also told by Luke, in Acts, beginning at 20:7.

Scholars debate whether the "first day" gathering in Acts 20 is referring to a Sabbath evening or a Sunday morning because they're focused on "journalistic history." They think that the most interesting "issue" with this story is whether Christians were

5 LUKE'S FIRST DAY

meeting on Saturday or Sunday and what that means for legitimizing the Christian practice of meeting on Sunday rather than Saturday. All power to them.

But most of their discussion misses the obvious point: Luke is a liturgical historian. And liturgical historians tell their readers *when* and *where* their stories take place in order to relate them to other meaningful stories that occur at *similar times* and *places*, and therefore to teach those readers how to commemorate those events in their liturgical assemblies. With that in mind, and knowing what we already know about the meaning of "the first day of the week," listen to this story:

> On the first day of the week (*de tē mia tōn sabbatōn*), when we were gathered together to break bread, Paul talked with them, intending to depart on the next day, and he prolonged his speech until midnight. There were many lamps in the upper room where we were gathered. And a young man named Eutychus, sitting at the window, sank into a deep sleep as Paul talked still longer. And being overcome by sleep, he fell down from the third story and was taken up dead. But Paul went down and bent over him, and taking him in his arms, said, "Do not be alarmed, for his life is in him." And when Paul had gone up and had broken bread and eaten, he conversed with them a long while, until daybreak, and so departed. And they took the youth away alive, and were not a little comforted. (20:7–12)

The first thing to notice about this passage is that Luke uses the exact same words to begin this story, *de tē mia tōn sabbatōn*, as he does the story of Jesus' resurrection in Luke 24. The first day of the week has become an immensely meaningful day for all the reasons discussed above. That phrase itself doesn't tell us exactly what the two stories have in common, but it's supposed to get readers to pay attention.

The second thing to notice is that this "first day" is not just the first day of any week, but the "first day of the week," just twelve days after the week of Unleavened Bread. It's not the day that directly follows the first Sabbath after Passover, like the day

SUNDAY

Jesus rises, but it's within the season of Firstfruits. Remember that the Feast of Firstfruits was fixed on the first day after the first Sabbath after Passover, but that *bikkurim* were accepted every day until the Feast of Booths (e.g. *m. bik* 1:6). Here's the text: "We sailed away from Philippi after the days of Unleavened Bread, and in five days we came to them at Troas, where we stayed for seven days. On the first day of the week …" (20:6–7). Notice that Luke is not just situating this story in the context of the weekly calendar, but in Israel's annual liturgical calendar. It's Firstfruits season, and his story about Jesus' resurrection has given us an appetite for resurrection stories.

The story begins comically. The room is full of light, so no one should be falling asleep. But Paul is talking for a *long time*, so who knows? Eutychus, the youth, had probably stayed up too late the previous night playing video games—those rascally youths—and he falls into a "deep sleep" and literally falls out a window to his death.

Okay, maybe it's a *dark* comedy.

Then Paul jumps into "first day resurrection" mode. We didn't even know it was a mode until Luke told this story. The first thing Paul does is to tell the congregation at Troas not to be alarmed (*thorubeō*, v. 10a) since there is still life in him. Same word Jesus used when He told Jairus that his daughter was only sleeping (*thorubeō*, Mark 5:39). Paul is raising Eutychus the same way Jesus raised Jairus' daughter. But it also reminds us of the *only other* "first day" gathering story told in the New Testament.

In Luke 24:36–53, Luke tells the story of Jesus gathering with His disciples on the "first day." He has already risen from the dead, and now they're all together. Just as Paul begins by telling the gathered believers not to be alarmed (Acts 20:10a), Jesus tells the gathered believers not to be troubled:

> As they were talking about these things, Jesus himself stood among them, and said to them, "Peace to you!" But they were startled and frightened and thought they saw a spirit. And he said to them, "Why are you troubled, and why do doubts arise in your hearts?" (Luke 24:36–38)

Paul's next step in Acts 20 is to give them a reason why they can believe that Eutychus is now living: "For his life is in him" (v. 10b). Jesus had presented a reason for them to believe He was alive, one that was also tactile: "'See my hands and my feet, that it is I myself. Touch me, and see. For a spirit does not have flesh and bones as you see that I have.' And when he had said this, he showed them his hands and his feet" (Luke 24:39–40).

The next clause in the Acts 20 story explains what Paul and the people did next: "And when Paul had gone up and had broken bread and eaten ..." (v. 11a). Jesus also eats with His disciples as soon as He gives evidence that He is alive: "And while they still disbelieved for joy and were marveling, he said to them, 'Have you anything here to eat?' They gave him a piece of broiled fish, and he took it and ate before them" (Luke 24:41–43).

Paul's sequence continues with conversation and departure: "And when Paul had gone up and had broken bread and eaten, he *conversed with them a long while*, until daybreak, and so *departed*" (Acts 20:11). The way Luke tells the story, Jesus does the same thing to end His "first day" gathering:

> *Then he said to them*, "These are my words that I spoke to you while I was still with you, that everything written about me in the Law of Moses and the Prophets and the Psalms must be fulfilled." Then he opened their minds to understand the Scriptures, and said to them, "Thus it is written, that the Christ should suffer and on the third day rise from the dead, and that repentance for the forgiveness of sins should be proclaimed in his name to all nations, beginning from Jerusalem. You are witnesses of these things. And behold, I am sending the promise of my Father upon you. But stay in the city until you are clothed with power from on high."
>
> And he led them out as far as Bethany, and lifting up his hands he blessed them. While he blessed them, *he parted from them and was carried up into heaven*. (Luke 24:44–51)

The scene in Acts 20 ends with Paul departing and the witnesses of Eutychus's resurrection sharing together in joy:

SUNDAY

"They took the youth away alive, and were not a little comforted" (v. 12). So with the disciples, eyewitnesses of Jesus' resurrection, in His absence: "And they worshiped him and returned to Jerusalem with great joy, and were continually in the temple blessing God" (Luke 24:52–53).

After Paul's resurrection of Eutychus, Luke focuses his narrative on describing where Paul sails next and then explaining the reason why he charts the course that he does: "he was hastening to be at Jerusalem, if possible, on the day of Pentecost" (Acts 20:16). Luke tells the story of Paul's resurrection of Eutychus (vv. 7–12) immediately following a reference to the Feast of Unleavened Bread (v. 6) and immediately preceding a reference to the day of Pentecost (vv. 13–16).

Like the story of Yahweh's resurrection of Jesus, Paul's resurrection of Eutychus is a "first day" Firstfruits story. Paul performs a resurrection that begins with a near quotation of Jesus' resurrection of Jairus' daughter and continues with an extraordinarily similar structure: He speaks words of comfort (Acts 20:10a; cf. Luke 24:36–38); provides evidence for the young person's being alive (Acts 20:10b; cf. Luke 24:39–40); eats (Acts 20:11a; Luke 24:41–43); converses until he departs (Acts 20:11b; Luke 24:44–51); and then leaves the witnesses in a state of comfort and joy (Acts 20:12; Luke 24:52–53).

Whether or not these correspondences provide enough evidence to make a journalistic claim about the timing and the character of early Christian gatherings, they do provide grounds for strengthening our claim about Luke's liturgical storytelling: For Luke, the "first day of the week," one between Passover and Pentecost, which corresponds with Firstfruits, is a New Testament holiday. That is, a "particular day of the calendar, especially a festival or fast day, designated for the historical or eschatological reference of analogous events."[7] Luke wants his readers to imagine Sunday as a day on which Christians gather, the dead are bodily resurrected, bread is broken, people converse, and hearts are comforted.

---

7. Stern, *Time and Process in Ancient Judaism*, 46.

6 THE SUBSTANCE

"Do this in remembrance of me."
Luke 22:19

"The substance belongs to Christ."
Colossians 2:17

In the previous chapters, I have argued that Sunday is the Church's commemorative holiday, instituted in the texts of the New Testament, forged out of renewed observations of the Sabbath, the Passover, and Firstfruits.

In Chapter 1, I demonstrated that the Sabbath—the weekly commemoration of Israel's Creation and Redemption in the Old Testament—is not just a "day," but is baked into Israel's other ceremonial and moral laws, like their whole Calendar (Lev 23) and their schedules for restoring persons and property (Exod 21; Lev 25; Deut 15), and that it is not just a day of "rest" for all persons but, for persons in positions of economic authority, it is a command to "release" their sons, daughters, servants, visitors, and animals unto rest.

In Chapter 2, I reflected on several ways in which conceiving of the Sabbath and the Passover as "commemorative holidays" and liturgical seasons of "eternal recurrence" suggests that we should investigate their meaning in Scripture. I argued that readers of Scripture should pay attention not only to texts of institution and fulfillment, but also to texts about their observation throughout history. I offered theses on the Old Testament's critical words, the genre of "festal speech," the ways in which presidential figures take up the work of the "fathers" in order to realize their aspirational values in history, and the adverbial phrases which some scholars call "time markers" and which frame historical narratives by relating them to external events.

In Chapter 3, I argued that Luke presents Jesus as receiving and renewing the institution of the Sabbath according to the same "Big Vision" that I presented in Chapter 1. The Sabbath remains a day of rest. But, as in the Old Testament, the Sabbath is a day, but it's not *just* a "day." It's the Year of the Lord's favor that Jesus proclaimed in Galilee at Nazareth. The Sabbath is not just about "rest" but about the ongoing triumph of Jesus, compelling the powers—visible and invisible—to acknowledge their duty to "keep" the Sabbath by proclaiming release. I also argued that Luke presents Jesus as both the kind of Sabbath-keeper who realizes Israel's vision for rest by rebuking the powers and proclaiming release, and the kind of festal speaker who characterizes both forgiveness and the love of enemies not as abstract moral principles but specifically as works of "release" and, therefore, of Sabbath-keeping. In his seven Sabbath stories, Luke presents his readers with a Jesus who teaches us how to keep the Sabbath truly.

In Chapter 4, I began with the observation that Jesus fulfills the Passover not only as the "lamb," but also as the "president" over the feast. As such, His "keeping" of the Passover stands in the great line of Passover presidents past: Moses, Joshua, Hezekiah, Josiah, and Ezra's Levites. When the Church's celebrants lift the Bread and the Cup of the New Covenant, which we do in imitation of Jesus, they imitate the One Man who was already lifting bread and cups in imitation of great men before Him. I argued

6 THE SUBSTANCE

that the way Scripture records its Passover stories suggests to its readers that the *meaning* of Passover has to do with commemorating Yahweh's great deliverance of Israel from Egypt on the eve of some moment of major transition in national history: leaving Sinai; entering Canaan; uniting the kingdom, renewing worship, and defeating Sennacherib; falling in battle to Neco, King of Egypt; and renewing Israel's rest at the completion of their Second Temple.

I also demonstrated that, largely for these reasons, Israel understood "Passover Time" as a time to expect some new kind of national deliverance. Jesus refocuses this general sense of Passover vigilance by delivering a new charge to be "ready" for His plunderous return, specifically for the Thief and the Banquet. The Church keeps the Passover rightly when we not only repeat Jesus' ritual, but when we gather up all the stories of God's deliverance, relate them to God's great deliverance out of death, and remind one another to be "ready" for God's next act of deliverance: whether it be release from prison, *à la* Peter in Acts 12, or the end of the age. Keeping the Eucharistic Rite, which is the way in which Jesus charges the Church to keep the Passover, abridges Church history, reminding us of our participation in Christ's death and resurrection in our baptisms; recalls the entire history of God's acts of deliverance; and prepares us for His next acts of deliverance, whatever they might be.

In Chapter 5, I explained that the "first day of the week" after the Passover is liturgical shorthand for the underappreciated Feast of Firstfruits. First, I characterized the rite according to Leviticus 23, Deuteronomy 26, and Israel's liturgical manuals and commentaries, and then I showed the ways in which Jesus' resurrection fulfills the themes of resurrection, harvest, and offering already present in Israel's understanding of the rite. That led to a brief study of the ways in which the New Testament authors, Paul, James, and John, use the word "firstfruits" (*aparchē*). For them, the figure of the "firstfruits" (*aparchē*; *bikkurim*) stands for the person or group of people who are the first to be converted, martyred, or otherwise "harvested" from among the rest of the people in the geographical region, or "field," to which they belong, in anticipation of a good harvest from that land. I established that the "firstfruits"—whether that refers to Jesus, the household of Stephanas, Epaenetus, the Jews in the Diaspora, or the 144,000 martyrs who follow the lamb—"sacralize" the others who have grown up alongside them and serve as evidence that Yahweh, the Vinedresser, will raise others up along with them. In short, the New Testament use of "firstfruits" illustrates that resurrection and conversion are not abstract and individualistic notions but liturgical principles, grounded and figured in Leviticus.

Finally, I reflected on the other two passages that include the term "the first day of the week." In the first one, Paul organizes the Corinthians' Sunday offerings along similar lines to the Firstfruits offering. Like the Firstfruits offering, the Sunday offering is prepared ahead of time, relatively unregulated, centralized in Jerusalem, related to possession of the land, and focused on the formation of the giver. In the second one, Luke tells another story whose narrative sequence matches the story of Jesus' resurrection: Paul speaks words of comfort, provides evidence of resurrection, enjoys food and conversation, and then takes his leave from the joyful company.

In the light of all this, I have concluded that, as do Leviticus and the rest of the Old Testament, the New Testament also institutes and develops a festal concept—the Christian Sunday—and that this concept is informed by three of the Old Testament's festal concepts: the Sabbath in its weekliness, commemorative quality, and ethical imaginativeness; the Passover in its liturgical abridgement of history, its record of the great acts of Yahweh through and with our fathers, and its call to be ready for the next act of deliverance; and Firstfruits, in its joyful celebration of God's ownership of the land and the ripeness of His harvest.

Jesus fulfills the Scriptures, including its entire festal tradition. The celebrant who calls the Church to keep Sundays according to the principle of Yahweh's—and Jesus'—Sabbath keeps Yahweh's charge to Moses to proclaim His festivals (Lev 23:4). And the congregation that keeps Sunday in its liturgical and ethical fullness, as displayed in the Scriptures and fulfilled in Christ, walks in the Spirit of Jesus.

As an Anglican clergyman, I am thankful to minister within an established liturgical tradition that, whether it realizes it or not, ritualizes each of these themes. The *Book of Common Prayer* prompts me to rest, to confess sins and proclaim absolution, to pray for my enemies and for the deliverance of the world, to forgive others of debts both moral and material, to commemorate Jesus' death and resurrection in the celebration of the Eucharist, to make offerings, and to feast in joy. It's all been in our book all along.

Whether or not you minister or worship within an established liturgical tradition, here are ten ways in which you can keep Sundays in the Spirit of Jesus:

1. Learn how to discern and rebuke the powers

When I read Luke's stories about Jesus, I don't see a man who "practices" "disciplines" of "rest" and "invites others" into "participation" in those disciplines. In short, I don't see a Sabbath Guru.

When I read Luke's stories about Jesus, I see a Sabbath *Hero* who "rebukes" (4:35), "rebukes" (4:39), and "rebukes" (4:41) the powers that bind the members of His household and prevent them from resting.

This reminds me of Paul's charge to Timothy to "preach the word," where one of the things he tells him to be ready to do, with "great patience and instruction," is to "rebuke" (2 Tim 4:1–2).

What Jesus does to the powers on the Sabbath is not exhaustive of what it means to rebuke. There are other kinds of rebuking. But this seems to be a special art that pastors ought to aspire to develop if they want to minister on Sunday and keep the Sabbath in the Spirit of Jesus.

How many sermons have you heard, and how many retreat lectures have you heard, exhorting you to rest? Is it the rhetorical burden of the pastor to talk about rest as a "practical application" or a "suggested practice"? I don't think so. I think, rather, that it is to discern the spirits and to spend Sundays rebuking the powers which bind people, proclaiming rest.

How do you rebuke Sin, Death, and Hell in a sermon? In a counseling session? When you are hearing a confession and offering absolution? In prayer ministry? On a spiritual retreat?

2. Proclaim release to your household

The synagogue official in Luke's seventh Sabbath story didn't know what the Sabbath was for (Luke 13:10–17), but Darius knew how to keep it (Ezra 6:8–10).

Why? I don't know. But it must have something to do with training in statecraft. As a premodern king, Darius understood the relationship between liturgical time and economics, and how that relationship bears on the formation of a religio-political community. (Would that all God's people minored in political science….)

Take the story of Jesus' care for that woman—the "daughter of Abraham," "afflicted" and "bound" for eighteen years by a spirit—as an icon of fatherhood and proclaim release to your own daughters. This is just another thing Paul tells Timothy: "He must manage his own household well … for if someone does not know how to manage his own household, how will he care for God's church?" (1 Tim 3:4–5).

The synagogue official serves as a warning to pastors. You, too, officiate a place of worship, and you, too, know that the Sabbath is for "rest." What you may from time to time forget is that, in the Scriptures, you are one of the "rulers" to whom *both* halves of the Sabbath Command are addressed. Like Pharaoh, and Moses, and Darius, and Jesus, and this guy.

For you, to keep the Sabbath Day holy requires that you proclaim release to those under your authority: to your spouse, to your children, to your volunteers, to your students, and to your staff.

You cannot proclaim release well in your church, nor can you admonish other "rulers" under your authority to grant rest if you are not practiced in this yourself.

6 THE SUBSTANCE

3. Discuss restoration with Zaccheus

The world, and the Church too, is thinking about the difficult ethical question of reparations, which largely refers to the state's financial- and land-based compensation of the descendants of those who are victims of slavery and *de jure* segregation.

Fundamental to the *theological* discussion about reparations is the question of what it means to "possess" land in the first place. And of fundamental value to a Christian understanding of "possession" is the Levitical notion of tenancy. Just a few verses down from the line that is etched into our Liberty Bell (Lev 25:10), Yahweh establishes a principle: "The land shall not be sold in perpetuity, for the land is mine. For you are strangers and sojourners with me. And in all the country you possess, you shall allow a redemption of the land" (vv. 23–24).

What role does the pastor have in discussions of reparations policy at the federal level? I suppose it depends on who you know.

For most of us, though, who don't belong to the same country club as our local state senator, the issue that people today refer to as "reparations" or "restitution" is more of an ethical issue of what to do with our privately-held capital than with state-owned land. The leader of any land- or capital-owning corporation—whether legally incorporated as a state or as a for-profit corporation—is figured as a king in Scripture and as a person to whom both halves of the Sabbath Command are addressed. So, like every other Christian who has deigned to write something on reparations, I would draw our attention to the private conversation between Jesus and Zaccheus.

We meet the Jesus who invites Himself into Zaccheus's home in Luke's Gospel, and in Luke's Gospel Jesus is the Lord of the Sabbath. Whatever the two of them say behind closed doors, the result of this personal visitation is twofold: first, a creative personal application of the Sabbath Command, in the form of fourfold restitution, as legislated in Exodus 22:1 ("he shall repay ... four sheep for a sheep"); and, second, the arrival of salvation to Zaccheus's household. Consider "Jesus' Visitation of Zaccheus" in Luke 19:1–10 another icon, or ministry model. Jesus brings the Law, which Zaccheus already knew, and makes it neither "too far" nor "too far off" (cf. Deut 30:11–14), inscribing it on his heart.

Perhaps Luke conceals the *content* of Jesus' discussion with Zaccheus in order to prevent his readers from identifying a univocal interpretive tradition or legal application of Exodus 22:1. What exactly did they discuss? Which Scriptures came up? Whose idea was a fourfold restitution? With which economic thoughts of the day did they interact?

The world is confused about reparation. Leviticus loves restoration, but it's hard to know how to apply its laws in every case. If you are a pastor and one of the "kings of the earth" comes under your authority and care, visit them and lead them into creative expressions of repentance and restitution. Discern with them the ways in which the Spirit may be calling them to restore persons and property, and so fulfill the Sabbath Command in the Spirit of Jesus.

4. Teach people how and why we proclaim "release" on Sundays

When the Bible introduces a holiday, it tells the people who keep it how to explain that holiday to children and to future generations.

Why does Israel rest on the Seventh Day?

Israel rests on the Seventh Day because Yahweh rested on the Seventh Day after He finished creating everything He created. And also because He brought them out of Egypt and promised to finish making them His new creation.

(That's the Level One answer. In Chapter 1 of this book, I offered a Level Two answer.)

Why does the Church worship on the first day of the week?

The Church worships on the first day of the week because that's the day on which Jesus rose from the dead, opened the Scriptures, spoke words of comfort, was known to His disciples in the breaking of the bread, and departed from His friends.

That's the Level One answer, and you already knew that.

6 THE SUBSTANCE

It has been the goal of the rest of this book to offer, at length, a Level Two answer to the questions, "What does Sunday mean?" and "Why do we do what we do on Sundays?" Every liturgical tradition has books and blogs dedicated to giving biblical and traditional warrant for each component of their liturgy, and I don't intend to reproduce any of that work here. Rather, I want to offer a series of imaginative touchpoints for providing your congregation with Level Two answers to the question, "Why do we do *this liturgical thing* on Sundays?" As an Anglican, I've taken an order of service from our prayer book tradition.

The Procession and Acclamation: We begin the abridged ritual reenactment of our national and civic history. Israel's holidays began *just as if* that gathered congregation had just walked out of Egypt and into the Promised Land. The Church begins our Sunday worship *just as if* we have immediately left the kingdom of darkness and entered the kingdom of heaven. That's why baptismal fonts and holy water dispensers are positioned at the back of the church.

The Collect of the Day and the Collect for Purity: Israel purged "the old leaven" on their way out of Egypt, but they knew from the beginning, as we do, that this ritually symbolized Yahweh's plan to purge the old leaven from their hearts.

The Scripture Lessons and the Holy Gospel: Jesus is the Founder and Sacred Hero of the Church, and we read His history as our own spiritual history before we commemorate the great death, resurrection, and ascension in which we participate—the life that is ours in Christ.

The Sermon: A presiding member of the congregation takes our sacred texts and, like a prophet *or* a king, gives a word that captures both the letter and the spirit of the text, that fits the occasion, and that presses the particular parochial body to embody the values of the kingdom, realized in Jesus and yet "lacking" (Col 1:24) and aspirational in His ecclesial body—more sermons like Frederick Douglass's "Fourth of July Speech."

The Creed: The Sabbath legislation identified Yahweh as

Creator of the World and Redeemer of Israel. After the President spoke at Passover, Israel rededicated herself to the exclusive and right worship of Yahweh, dismantling idols. The Church identifies the Triune God as Creator and Redeemer and rededicates herself to right worship.

The Prayers of the People: Just as the early Church expected Yahweh to continue to deliver His people according to the pattern He established when He delivered them from Egypt, and kept up a watchful vigilance that included praying for Peter's release, the Church continues to pray for various forms of deliverance in the world. And because Jesus taught that the Sabbath principle of "release" extends even to love of one's enemies and the remission of debts, we pray for our enemies and promise to forgive one another.

The Confession of Sin and the Absolution: Jesus showed that it is not only permissible to perform works of release, but that this is what makes the Sabbath "for man" in the first place. The President of the congregation, official of the synagogue, and head of the local household of God, empowers God's people to rebuke and renounce the powers and offers a word of rebuke and release himself, on their behalf.

The Passing of the Peace: Peace is the fruit of release, remission, and absolution.

The Offering: The Firstfruits tradition offers the Church a template for responding to God's gift of land and settlement with an offering of various kinds of firstfruits. The controlling metaphor is that when seeds are planted in faith and die, God raises fruit from them. Those seeds may be literal seeds, seed money, or generative ideas. Ultimately, they are our bodies and souls. When we willingly submit to the death of baptism and pick up Christ's cross to follow Him, we sow our bodies in faith that God will not only raise us up and ripen the fruits of the Spirit within us, but that He will raise up a greater harvest around us.

The Great Thanksgiving: The President abridged Israel's history in the Passover and invited all landowning Israelites to repeat it in the Firstfruits Creed at Deuteronomy 26:5–10. The Firstfruits

Creed succinctly explained why Israel kept time by ritually offering up sacrifices of thanksgiving. The Church's formal prayers of thanksgiving likewise abridge and crystallize the history of our redemption, and they explain why we offer up the sacrifices of the new covenant: bread, wine, and ourselves chief among them.

The Words of Institution: The President did this at both Passover and Firstfruits.

Receiving Communion: Both the Passover and Firstfruits consisted of ritual meals. The stories of great Passover Observances and the instructions for Firstfruits provide imaginative data for understanding the significance of corporate eating during national holidays. Consider also the significance of the meals eaten by Jesus and Paul in the New Testament's five "first day of the week" narratives.

Post-Communion: After the Passover, Israel did great things, and so the Church prays for "strength and courage" to "do the work" given us. Meanwhile, after thanksgiving offerings, like the Firstfruits offering, Leviticus required that there be no food left over, and so celebrating clergy in the Church will consume the remaining bread and wine (7:15–18).

Consuming the sacrament is usually the purview of a deacon or a priest in the Anglican tradition. But leftover bread and wine in other traditions, or leftover "fellowship hour" food, could be distributed to needy families or even church members who have particular individual devotion to the Eucharist.

To be clear, this is by no means a truthful history of how this liturgy was constructed, nor does it offer a Level One answer for why each component of the liturgy was included. All this does is offer a series of imaginative touchpoints between our Eucharistic rite and normative liturgical timekeeping in Israel. In doing so, this can help you use the Bible to explain how and why the Church keeps the Sabbath Command in its fullness on Sundays.

SUNDAY

5. Fold your personal and historical thanksgivings into the Great Thanksgiving

After Jesus formally fulfilled the Passover, which was a cumulative celebration of all that God had done to deliver Israel, God gives at least one "Passover Encore." Christians pray for Peter's release from prison during the Passover, and then God sends another angel to release him according to the pattern established in Israel's deliverance from Egypt and fulfilled in Jesus' deliverance from death and the Church's deliverance from the kingdom of darkness.

It is curious that, even though Jesus fulfilled the concept of Passover-time expectancy, Christians didn't stop praying for and expecting earthly acts of deliverance from Yahweh during Passover time. And God didn't stop delivering.

Take this as a cue to press into the organic relationship between *petitions and thanksgivings for earthly acts of deliverance* and *the Eucharistic commemoration*.

In the Anglican liturgy, room is made for this in two separate places, although the relationship is not made explicit. First, in the Prayers of the People, we pray for people like Peter, and then we thank God for the things He has done. Here's what the book says:

> **Reader**: For all those who are in trouble, sorrow, need, sickness, or any other adversity
> [especially _____].
> **R**: Lord, in your mercy:
> **People**: *Hear our prayer.*
> **R**: For all those who have departed this life in the certain hope of the resurrection
> [especially _____,] in thanksgiving let us pray.
> **R**: Lord, in your mercy:
> **P**: *Hear our prayer.*

Additional petitions may be added. Thanksgivings may also be invited.

6 THE SUBSTANCE

Minutes later, the Celebrant offers a prayer called "The Great Thanksgiving" on behalf of the Church, for God's deliverance from death and the powers. Here it is in one version:

> Holy and gracious Father: In your infinite love you made us for yourself; and when we had sinned against you and become subject to evil and death, you, in your mercy, sent your only Son Jesus Christ into the world for our salvation. By the Holy Spirit and the Virgin Mary he became flesh and dwelt among us. In obedience to your will, he stretched out his arms upon the Cross and offered himself once for all, that by his suffering and death we might be saved. By his resurrection he broke the bonds of death, trampling Hell and Satan under his feet. As our great high priest, he ascended to your right hand in glory, that we might come with confidence before the throne of grace.

The Roman Catholic tradition is even more explicit in their Eucharistic Rite. In one version, their Missal folds the concerns of the "Prayers of the People" into the prefatory section of the prayer:

> To you, therefore, most merciful Father, we make humble prayer and petition through Jesus Christ, your Son, our Lord: that you accept and bless these gifts, these offerings, these holy and unblemished sacrifices, which we offer you firstly for your holy catholic Church. Be pleased to grant her peace, to guard, unite and govern her throughout the whole world, together with your servant [N.] our Pope and [N.] our Bishop, and all those who, holding to the truth, hand on the catholic and apostolic faith.

Another version gathers the intercessions of the people—first of the whole world and then of the Church—in the penultimate section of the Eucharistic prayer:

> May this Sacrifice of our reconciliation, we pray, O Lord, advance the peace and salvation of all the world. Be pleased to confirm in faith and charity your pilgrim Church on earth, with your servant [N.] our Pope and [N.] our Bishop, the Order of Bishops, all the clergy, and the entire people you have gained for your own.

>Listen graciously to the prayers of this family, whom you have summoned before you.

All I have endeavored to argue here is that the Celebrant need not instruct the congregation to separate their vigilance and commemorations—expressed in petitions and thanksgivings—for instances of earthly deliverance from their vigilance for Christ's Parousia and their commemoration of His Passion.

God drowned Pharaoh and his army, and He freed Peter from prison. Not only may the Church continue to pray for other earthly acts of deliverance that follow that pattern, but the Celebrant may stand in line with the Passover Presidents of Scripture and explicitly fold all of those petitions and thanksgivings of the people into the Great Thanksgiving.

All things hold together in Christ anyway.

6. Keep the Church's Calendar

This isn't a book on the Church's Calendar; it's a book about Sunday. But the foregoing chapters permit me to say two things, almost speaking out of both sides of my mouth:

First, keeping Sunday is enough. Jesus fulfilled the Law, and the rites that characterize Sunday worship provide the Church with ample opportunity to commemorate all that Israel's calendar meant to them. Sunday is a crystallization of Israel's calendar.

Second, keeping the Church's Calendar isn't unbiblical. Sunday proliferates. Israel had a calendar, and the Church matches it fairly closely. In place of the Sabbath, we keep Sunday. In place of Unleavened Bread, we keep Holy Week. They kept the Day of Atonement; we keep Good Friday. They had Firstfruits around the same time; we end Holy Week with Easter, which, like Firstfruits, begins another fifty-day season that ends with Pentecost. We agree that Firstfruits and Pentecost are "harvest" festivals. We don't keep Tabernacles, remembering that we wandered in a desert before we got houses, but we do keep Lent, remembering that humanity was "but dust" before we were clothed in bodies and that our bodies are still tabernacles (Psa 103:14; 2 Cor 5:4).

Their holidays were clustered in Months 1 and 7; we keep Christmas and Easter six-ish months apart. Israel was inspired to add Purim when Haman was hanged; and some branches of the Church added Christ the King in 1925 to tell Mussolini that Jesus was King of Kings.

Keeping the Church's Calendar acknowledges that the shape of a human life under the sun today is not fundamentally unlike life under the sun back then, even if far fewer of us are farmers. We are born into a historical community, many of us marry and have children, and we die. We endure four seasons a year and mark the solar year, the fiscal year, and the academic year with our own cultural traditions anyway.

Keeping a common calendar offers people a common passage through life. Keep the Church's Calendar to throw in your lot with the people of God throughout time and space. Everyone goes back to the gym in January or starts writing their term papers in May.

Take the common, human impulse to engage in a temporary season of discipline, and sanctify that impulse by practicing Lent. Lots of people wish the holidays didn't move so fast; others hate the over-sentimentalization of a painful season. Call people to keep Advent.

7. Keep the Federal Calendar

This isn't a book about the Church's Calendar, and it's even less a book about the United States' Federal Calendar. But understanding Sunday in the context of Scripture's holiday tradition gives the Church some tools to reflect on what it means to participate in their own nation's festal calendar.

Although we have common cultural customs—cookouts in May, fireworks in July, pumpkin spice lattes in late September, family dinners in November—the United States doesn't have a normative festal principle. In that vacuum, some people, like Jeroboam, invent new holidays out of their own hearts in order to divide people. Other people, like Edward Covey, invent traditions designed to suppress the members of their own household. Most people keep holidays according to their own traditions and sentimental values. In those cases, often the worst thing that happens is that people experience them as lonely or sad (e.g., the motherless on Mothers' Day and the lonely on Thanksgiving).

In a nation without a normative festal principle, the Church has an opportunity to teach the world how to harmonize its holidays to the Sabbath. As a people freed from the kingdom of darkness but still wrestling with the influence of sin, we know how to celebrate the Fourth of July. As a people adopted into the family of God while experiencing imperfect relationships with our families of origin, we know how to celebrate Thanksgiving. As a people promised the earth and its fruits as an inheritance despite having uneven distributions of wealth, we know how to celebrate the beginning of a harvest season.

To take one holiday that many churches haven't thought much about because it has so recently been established as a federal holiday, consider Juneteenth. How could our churches harmonize that holiday according to Scripture and the Sabbath principle?

Juneteenth is a holiday, observed annually on June 19 since 1865 and federally established in 2021. It commemorates the date on which Union Army General Gordon Granger fulfilled Lincoln's Emancipation Proclamation by proclaiming emancipation in Texas, the last of the states in the Confederacy to formally dissolve institutional slavery. Due to its obvious resonances with the institution described in Leviticus 25 and fulfilled in Luke 4, the holiday's original name was Jubilee Day.

These newly-emancipated and enfranchised Texans were still legally prohibited from gathering in public parks. But the holiday grew in 1872 when Black leaders raised $1,000 to purchase ten acres in Houston, specifically *for* Jubilee Day celebrations. It grew even greater in 1898 when an estimated crowd of 30,000 gathered in Booker T. Washington Park, which was purchased and dedicated to celebrating Juneteenth.

Purchasing land to celebrate emancipation sounds like Moses' instructions about the development of the Passover: "Today, in the month of Abib, you are going out. And when Yahweh brings you into the land of the Canaanites, the Hittites, the

Amorites, the Hivites, and the Jebusites, which he swore to your fathers to give you, a land flowing with milk and honey, you shall keep this service in this month" (Exod 13:4–5). From the earliest years, this particular historical community whose leaders purchased this land began telling and keeping their history in a way that deeply resembled Israel's.

This clarifies one way in which citizenship in the United States is unlike citizenship in Israel. In Israel, the experience of emancipation from Egypt and possession of the Promised Land became a unifying, normative experience for an entire nation. Looking back with contemporary categories, we might call the Passover a holiday for both a particular ethnic group and an entire nation. In the United States, Juneteenth was an ethnic holiday long before it became a federal holiday, and it is not immediately clear how U.S. citizens who are not members of that particular ethnic group ought to keep that feast. That's a lesson: Keeping holidays is more complicated in modern multi-ethnic nation-states.

As your church, or the people in your church, consider how to acknowledge the United States' newest holiday this year, here are a few reflections on the Bible's holidays:

First, unlike the United States' holidays, Israel's primary holidays were established legally before they were established culturally. Yahweh didn't respond to cultural traditions from within different corners of Israel by institutionalizing them 156 years after the fact. He instituted the Sabbath and the Passover Himself, and His immediate expectation was that all Israelites would celebrate them together.

Second, Yahweh's festal program was designed for unity from the outset. Keeping Yahweh's Sabbath was a sign of being a true Israelite; keeping the Passover meant identifying oneself with Israel's history, and it became a sign of national unity during eras of division.

Frederick Douglass argued that the Fourth of July is "yours, not mine," but he argues this contingently. By the end of his speech, he expresses what he calls "optimism" that the holiday may one day celebrate the freedom it aspires to celebrate:

SUNDAY

"There are forces in operation, which must inevitably work the downfall of slavery." Passover and the Fourth of July purposed, by original *design*, to be for all people to celebrate. To the extent that they do not meet their nation's aspirations, the holiday gives the nation's prophets an occasion to speak a word of moral correction. A federal holiday like Mother's Day, on the other hand, was only ever meant to celebrate mothers.

Three, Israel's calendar already contains conditions for who ought to celebrate certain holidays and when. Take, for example, the Feast of Firstfruits. Yahweh instituted the holiday at Sinai (Lev 23), but He did not permit Israel to celebrate it until they arrived in Canaan (Josh 5). Even then, Israel's own interpretation of Deuteronomy 26:10 divided Israelites into tiers and restricted their participation in the ritual portions of the festal law. For example, landowning Israelites could recite the clause: "this ground, which you, O Yahweh, have given *me*." People who had bought trees could offer *bikkurim* but not recite the clause (cf. *m. bik*. 1: 2, 4–11). Some Israelites could do neither. The Old Testament and Israel's liturgical tradition offer models for tiered participation in historically significant holidays.

Four, unlike Yahweh, the United States' federal government does not encode ritual scripts into their legal holidays. Nothing requires American citizens to barbecue on Memorial Day, shoot fireworks on the Fourth, or eat turkey on Thanksgiving. Our only legal requirements are economic: Some kinds of corporations *must* provide their workers with a fixed day of paid time off; other kinds *may*.

What should your church do? There are lots of good answers. Here are a few:

You could supplement your "Prayers of the People" rite with prayers of thanksgiving for the deliverance that Juneteenth commemorates.

You could rededicate yourselves to the heroic work of proclaiming liberty, like Jesus (cf. Luke) and General Granger (ca. 1865).

You could take up an offering, like Cyrus, to give to a community organization that wants to buy land, or just host a barbecue.

Take an inventory of the holidays your church acknowledges or celebrates, as well as the ones it avoids. Our membership in particular ethnic and legal bodies within history requires that we respond to the festal time kept by those bodies. The Scriptures—in their institution narratives, legal and ritual texts, commemoration narratives, festal speeches, discussions of festal traditions, and fulfillment narratives—provide ample tools for thinking with theological nuance and creativity about our participation in those commemorative holidays.

This kind of theological nuance and creativity prepares pastors to be "brought before kings" (Matt 10:18). In the meantime, thank God for the unifying potential of Sunday, and of Good Friday and Easter, a Christian festal tradition of diverse expression, kept by the Church throughout the world.

8. Learn how to preach from reading great festal speakers

Like it or not, because Sunday is a commemorative holiday for a historical body and because we take a history book as our Holy Scriptures, the Sunday sermon is a festal speech, and preachers are festal orators.

Find the Frederick Douglass speeches I quoted at length and read them in full. Buy a book of Abraham Lincoln's and Winston Churchill's speeches. Read through the annual "State of the Union" addresses or "Inaugural" Addresses.

St. Augustine, who wrote the Church's first great textbook on Christian oratory, was himself an appreciative student of the speeches of statesmen. He especially liked Cicero. Be like Augustine; read Cicero!

What statesmen know is that even with a sacred text in front of them, which ought to be understood both in its letter and in its spirit, they are addressing a particular body of people at a particular point in history and that there are certain annual occasions for using canonical texts for reflecting on how their sacred history comes to bear on the present moment.

SUNDAY

If all Sundays are created equal, it is difficult to single out one particular Sunday to give a "State of the Union" address, as it were. It is often easier to exegete the given text and communicate its Big Idea™.

Christmas Eve is when visitors come. But consider taking Easter Sunday, or even Good Friday, and speaking less like a graduate student, less like a therapist, less like a basketball coach—though many pastors serve formally or informally in all three of these roles—and more like a president.

9. Forgive sins

Pastors are called upon to say lots of words. Lots of kinds of words. And to do lots of listening. This is by no means novel, but it seems important to end with a simple word—one that was never in dispute and one that doesn't require profound insight into the Sabbath: You keep the Sabbath by forgiving sins.

Jesus' parable about the unforgiving servant—forgiven of a great debt by the king, yet unwilling to forgive the substantially smaller debt of one of his own servants—is a Sabbatical parable. What man, freed from bondage in Egypt, has the gall to say Pharaoh's line: "I will not let you go"? One who has not learned to keep the Sabbath truly.

To forgive debt is to proclaim release, and to proclaim release is to grant rest. Granting rest is at the heart of keeping the Sabbath. If we keep the calendar and engage the holidays and teach the liturgy and obey the command to rest, but have not forgiveness, we have not kept the Sabbath.

Continue to practice forgiving sins by doing the things that pastors do: Hear private confessions, offer words of absolution and comfort after corporate liturgical confessions, require your Church not just to *know* the Lord's Prayer but to pray it together every week.

10. Keep the feast

The goal of this book is not to persuade pastors to revise or to edit their tradition's liturgy.

In short, my claim is that Sunday is Yahweh's appointed time and that pastors, like Moses, ought boldly to stand in the shoes of Israel's presidents and call God's people to worship—I hope, with richer appreciation and with imaginative courage.